Against
THE TIDE

Against THE TIDE

*Immigrants, Day Laborers, and
Community in Jupiter, Florida*

SANDRA LAZO DE LA VEGA
and
TIMOTHY J. STEIGENGA

THE UNIVERSITY OF WISCONSIN PRESS

The University of Wisconsin Press
1930 Monroe Street, 3rd Floor
Madison, Wisconsin 53711-2059
uwpress.wisc.edu

3 Henrietta Street
London WC2E 8LU, England
eurospanbookstore.com

Printed in the United States of America

Library of Congress Cataloging-in-Publication Data

Lazo de la Vega, Sandra.
Against the tide : immigrants, day laborers, and community in Jupiter, Florida / Sandra
Lazo de la Vega and Timothy J. Steigenga.
p.   cm.
Includes bibliographical references and index.
ISBN 978-0-299-29104-4 (pbk. : alk. paper) — ISBN 978-0-299-29103-7 (e-book)
1. Immigrants—Social conditions—Florida—Jupiter. 2. Immigrants—Services for—
Florida—Jupiter. 3. Day laborers—Services for—Florida—Jupiter. 4. Community
centers—Florida—Jupiter. 5. Jupiter (Fla.)—Emigration and immigration—
Social aspects. I. Steigenga, Timothy J., 1965– II. Title.
HV4012.J87L39   2013
362.89´9120840975932—dc23
2012018534

CONTENTS

ILLUSTRATIONS

ABBREVIATIONS

ABC	American Baptist Churches
AFL-CIO	American Federation of Labor and Congress of Industrial Organizations
CIP	Community Investment Program
CROS Ministries	Christians Reaching Out to Society Ministries
DHS	Department of Homeland Security
DR-CAFTA	Dominican Republic–Central America Free Trade Agreement
DREAM Act	Development, Relief, and Education for Alien Minors Act
ESL	English as a second language
FAIR	Federation for American Immigration Reform
FAU	Florida Atlantic University
FBI	Federal Bureau of Investigation
FCC	Federal Communications Commission
FEMA	Federal Emergency Management Agency
FLIC	Florida Immigrant Coalition
FLIMEN	Floridians for Immigration Enforcement
GDP	gross domestic product
IBEW	International Brotherhood of Electrical Workers
ICE	Immigration and Customs Enforcement
INCEDES	Central American Institute for Social Studies and Development

INS	Immigration and Naturalization Service
JNAIL	Jupiter Neighbors against Illegal Labor
JNRC	(El Sol) Jupiter's Neighborhood Resource Center
JPD	Jupiter Police Department
LACC	Latin American and Caribbean Center
NDLON	National Day Labor Organizing Network
PBSC	Palm Beach State College
PEACE	People Engaged in Active Community Efforts
SAT	Scholastic Aptitude Test
TOJ	town of Jupiter
TPS	Temporary Protective Status
USCIS	United States Citizenship and Immigration Services (INS)
VISTA	Volunteers in Service to America

Against
THE TIDE

Introduction

By 6:00 a.m. one morning in the summer of 2001, almost two hundred men stood in clusters around trees and vehicles and on the front porches lining Center Street, in Jupiter, Florida. As a pickup truck slowed down and came to a stop along the road, a group of men surged toward it and crowded around, all trying to speak to the driver. A number of them climbed into the truck bed while another negotiated their hourly rate. Within minutes, most of them again scrambled out and the truck pulled away with a crew of three holding onto their baseball caps, headed for a day's work on a construction site. The rest of the group slowly retreated from the roadside and resumed their positions, anxiously awaiting the next vehicle that might bring the opportunity for work.

The majority of the men lining Center Street that day were immigrants from Guatemala and Mexico who had recently moved into the apartment complexes and duplexes nearby. Surrounding Center Street are some of Jupiter's long-standing residential neighborhoods: Pine Gardens North, Pine Gardens South, Eastview Manor, Jupiter Plantation, and Jupiter River Estates. One of the residents from Pine Gardens North also rose early on that summer morning, hoping to go for a jog around the neighborhood before the temperatures soared into the nineties. As she turned the corner onto Center Street, she took in the scene at a glance but was determined to go on with her run. As her path took her past the group of men in front of the apartments, she could not help but feel uncomfortable. Not only were the faces she saw new to the neighborhood but the group of mostly young Hispanic men also spoke a language she could not understand. She tried not to look too much at the men, who continued to talk among themselves. One man said something to her in what sounded like English, but she couldn't make out his words exactly. Frustrated and somewhat intimidated, the jogger turned around and headed back toward her home.

Versions of this scenario were unfortunately frequent in Jupiter prior to 2006. Jupiter is a relatively small coastal town located on the northern edge of Palm Beach County. The area's beautiful beaches and golf courses make it a popular vacation and retirement destination. Throughout the late 1990s and 2000s, Jupiter experienced significant economic growth, creating an increased demand for construction workers, landscapers, and other service-industry laborers. Like that of many other small communities around the Southeast, Jupiter's growth coincided with an influx of immigrants, primarily from Central America and Mexico. As in many other such towns, residents and policy makers in the town initially struggled to understand and address the issues raised by a growing community of immigrants, many of whom were unauthorized.[1]

In the late 1990s and early 2000s the most visible manifestation of Jupiter's growing immigrant population was the group of day laborers who gathered each day to seek work along Center Street. Local contractors throughout Palm Beach and Martin counties and private homeowners in Jupiter knew where to find willing workers. But the open-air labor market soon began to generate problems for town authorities, as more and more local residents "expressed concerns related to safety, depreciation of property values, and trespassing" (Town Council Minutes, December 17, 2002). Following a series of complaints in 2001 and 2002, Jupiter's mayor asked the Police Department to issue a report on the situation. The section titled "PROBLEM" in the 2003 Jupiter police report noted, "Subjects gather in front of, behind and to the side of [several addresses around Center Street] in hopes they will be selected for work by landscaping companies or private citizens who pick up workers for their individual lawn needs." The report also noted that several attempts had been made to address the situation, including the erection of "No Trespassing" signs, calls to the Immigration and Naturalization Service (INS), and attempts to enlist local businesses to provide an alternate location for the day laborers. The conclusion of the report summarized the issue as follows.

The Police Department's problem, as a law enforcement agency, is the numerous calls we receive from citizens who are upset with the presence of the Guatemalans and Mexicans who stand along the sidewalks on Center Street waiting to be picked up for employment. . . . One of our officers who specifically is assigned to this patrol zone early on pinpointed the real problem: "We are fighting *against* the residents of 1600 Center Street [the address of an apartment complex where a large number of the residents are Guatemalan immigrants] rather than trying to work *with* them." We have made great strides in opening up dialogue with the Guatemalan community, but there is still a feeling of mistrust on the part of the residents.

While many localities around the United States have witnessed ugly confrontations and even violence in the face of similar issues, a coalition of immigrants, local neighborhood residents, students, and town representatives in Jupiter came together to mediate community tensions by successfully moving the informal labor market and associated problems to a clean and organized structure that provides a critical bridge between the immigrant and native populations of the town. In a few short years, the town not only found a positive solution to the very real neighborhood and quality-of-life problems outlined in the police report but also began to lay the groundwork for a long-term process of immigrant integration. El Sol, Jupiter's Neighborhood Resource Center, costs Jupiter taxpayers almost nothing and returns an estimated quarter of a million dollars in services annually to the local community.[2]

This book recounts the process of how El Sol was established, how it has engaged the residents of Jupiter in the two-way process of immigrant integration, and how it has come to serve as a model for other communities seeking a positive public policy solution to the problems associated with rapid, and frequently unauthorized, migration.

The Role of the Authors

As one of the individuals responsible for founding El Sol and its predecessor, Corn Maya Inc., Professor Timothy Steigenga was present at most of the meetings and events recounted in this book. He served on the board and the executive committee of El Sol until 2011 and continues to serve as a board member for Corn Maya Inc. and as a volunteer for El Sol. For the majority of the period covered in the book he also served as a co-principal investigator on two grants from the Ford Foundation, focusing on the study of Mexican, Guatemalan, and Brazilian immigrants in Florida and Georgia. Under the auspices of the Ford grants he had the opportunity to travel and conduct further research in Guatemala, and to work with Guatemalan researchers in conducting focus groups and interviews in Jupiter. Sandra Lazo de la Vega was also actively engaged with Corn Maya Inc. and El Sol, serving as the president of the Corn Maya student group on the Florida Atlantic University campus in Jupiter and as the primary liaison for student teachers of English as a second language (ESL) classes at El Sol. This book purposefully and self-consciously integrates our own experiences and relationships with the people involved into the broader story of El Sol.

In addition to our direct personal experiences, we conducted extensive interviews in 2011 with key figures from the town, its neighborhoods, and the groups involved in the process of opening and running El Sol. As much as possible, we have attempted to allow the major actors to provide their perspective in their own words, using direct quotations from interviews, transcripts of Town Council meetings, flyers, e-mails, and other primary sources collected between 2002 and 2011. In some instances, punctuation has been added for clarity. Interviews conducted in Spanish were translated into English by the authors.

A theme that runs throughout the book is trust. Had we come to this topic as "outside" researchers, there is little chance that we would have been able to have the frank and wide-ranging discussions on which this book is based. From the local authorities to neighborhood residents to members of the immigrant community, we entered the interview process with previously established personal and professional relationships built up over years of working together. All of our interviewees were provided the opportunity to review the portions of their interviews contained in the book for factual accuracy and were given the opportunity to retract any statements considered inaccurate.

Our account weaves together our own firsthand knowledge of events with information drawn from town and newspaper archives and in-depth interviews to tell the story of El Sol and reflect on its meaning in the context of the current immigration debate. We decided to write this book precisely because we believe the experience of El Sol holds lessons and insights that extend far beyond the specific case of Jupiter and the issue of day labor. While the media have tended to focus on the law-enforcement side of local immigration activism, a number of towns and localities around the United States have adopted integrative policies toward immigrants similar to those developed in Jupiter. It is our hope that Jupiter's story can provide insights useful for other communities struggling with similar issues. The outlines of Jupiter's story are likely to resonate with those who live in similar new destinations for Latino immigration elsewhere.

Context and Conflict in New Destinations

Over the past few decades, immigrants coming to the United States from Latin America arrived primarily in specific gateway cities in California, Texas, Arizona, New York, and Florida. In Florida most immigrants initially went to Miami, where they were greeted with a hospitable linguistic environment due to the well-established Cuban community. Hispanic immigrants then began migrating to places beyond Miami and Dade County. Palm Beach County has become home to a significant number of them, especially in Lake Worth and other cities in the central and southern portions of the county. Jupiter's immigrant population began to grow rapidly in the mid to late 1990s as well. The town's rapid demographic change is evident in census figures and other data: in 1990 Jupiter's population was 24,986, of which less than 3 percent was Hispanic; in 2000 the population had grown to 39,328, of which 7.3 percent was Hispanic; and the 2005–9 American Community Survey put Jupiter's population at 49,442, of which Hispanics comprised an estimated 14.1 percent (6,947). In 2010 the absolute number of Hispanics in Jupiter held steady at 6,993, though declining somewhat proportionally to 12.7 percent of the 55,156 total.

The rapid influx of large groups of Hispanic immigrants into new destinations across the United States has raised a series of challenges for communities with no previous large-scale immigration experience. In particular, these communities have struggled with issues of reception, resources, and ethnic relations. Furthermore, immigrants within these new destinations have often moved into residential and frequently suburban communities, drawn by a growing demand for their labor in the construction and service industries. As the number of immigrants grew, suburban communities began to experience rising levels of tension and conflicts at the local level. Day labor frequently became a "hot-button" issue, stoking deep-seated community concerns about unauthorized immigration.

In Hazleton, Pennsylvania, for example, tensions between longtime Hazleton residents and the immigrant community reached a boiling point following a shooting, for which two unauthorized immigrants from the Dominican Republic were arrested. Hazleton mayor Lou Barletta drew a strong link between illegal immigration and crime committed in the town. Following the shooting the mayor declared, "Illegal immigrants are destroying the city. I don't want them here, period."[3] Despite the lack of evidence to support the mayor's claims about the link between immigrants and crime, the Town Council approved the Hazleton Illegal Immigration and Reform Act Ordinance in July of 2006. This act declared English the official language of Hazleton, established fines for people who rented housing to unauthorized individuals, and required that all businesses operating within Hazleton submit an affidavit affirming that they did not employ unauthorized workers.[4] The mayor and Town Council took particular aim at unauthorized workers, especially day laborers, because their presence caused people to be "afraid to walk down the street."[5] Although the Hazleton ordinance was challenged in court and never went into effect, it generated significant national attention and many discussions of similar ordinances in other communities.

As in Hazleton, the issue of day labor became a flashpoint in Herndon, a small town in Fairfax County, Virginia. Residents of Herndon complained bitterly to town authorities about the day laborers who gathered at a local 7-Eleven seeking work. Residents complained about the crowds, and in 2005 a total of twenty-one people were arrested for nuisance crimes such as public drinking and trespassing.[6] Ultimately, the Herndon Town Council voted in August 2005 to fund a hiring site where day laborers could be picked up. It also passed a no-solicitation ordinance prohibiting workers from gathering on the street or in the 7-Eleven parking lot. The town of Herndon allocated funds for a hiring site, but in 2006 the mayor and two council members who had supported the opening of the center lost their positions to candidates who promised the electorate that they would shut it down. Finally in 2007, just twenty-one months after the center opened, the Town Council voted in favor of shutting it down "instead of complying with a judge's ruling that the site must be open to all residents, including those who might be illegal immigrants."[7]

The issue of day labor was also at the center of the controversy in the infamous case of Farmingville, New York. As Farmingville had become home to hundreds of Latin American immigrants, tensions between them and native-born residents heated up. Some residents formed an official group to oppose the newcomers, and soon this group began attracting support from hate groups. Tensions continued to escalate, and in the summer of 2000 two immigrants were beaten nearly to death by four teenagers. In another incident, in 2003, the home of a Mexican family was set on fire by local teenagers; fortunately no one was injured. The perpetrators, when they were caught, said they had burned the house down *because* they knew that immigrants lived there. In the end Farmingville was unable to resolve its day labor issue, and the climate of violence and intolerance continued. In 2004 the events in Farmingville were the subject of an acclaimed documentary, *Farmingville*.

THE EL SOL ALTERNATIVE

As in Hazleton, Herndon, Farmingville, and many other communities, day labor ignited the original controversy in Jupiter. Unlike Herndon, however, the labor center that opened in Jupiter to address the local problems remains open and continues to prosper. The primary goal of El Sol when it opened in 2006 was to get the day laborers off the street. The center, in this respect, has succeeded completely and has grown beyond the expectations of its founders and supporters. Today El Sol is an established social service agency that enjoys widespread support among Jupiter residents, media, and politicians.

Open seven days a week, El Sol's mission is framed in terms of improving the quality of life for all of Jupiter's residents. El Sol pursues this mission by organizing and supervising the day labor market in a controlled and sanitary atmosphere; educating day laborers and contractors about their rights and responsibilities; assisting immigrants to become an active and integrated part of the larger community; building bridges between Jupiter's different ethnic, cultural, and religious groups; and providing occupational training, language and literacy instruction, counseling, health education, and legal and other services to individuals in need. Thus, El Sol provides both a critical set of services for immigrants and a way for local residents who volunteer at the center to conceive of immigration in more human terms. Since El Sol was founded in 2006, three other labor centers have opened in South Florida based on the El Sol model. Although one of those centers recently closed (in Lake Worth), El Sol continues to receive requests from other localities about its practices and programs. The center is now a fixture in the Jupiter community, but the process of establishing it was a long and arduous one.

"If You Build It, They Will Come"

The opening of El Sol was part of a larger set of policies designed to resolve the tensions and quality-of-life issues arising in neighborhoods where Jupiter's newest immigrants were concentrated. The initial discussion about whether or not to open El Sol, however, drew the town into a much larger immigration debate. One of the objections to El Sol commonly raised before its opening was the claim "If you build it, they will come." In other words, if you create a center designed to serve the immigrant community the effect will be to attract more immigrants. Subsequent experience, however, has proved such worries unfounded. While the center opened in the midst of a rapid influx of immigration, the total number of Hispanics in the town has not significantly increased since; Jupiter's Hispanic population has essentially remained flat since the mid-2000s at just under seven thousand individuals. The center, however, did draw another group to Jupiter: politicians and pundits seeking to gain political advantage by exploiting the issue of illegal immigration. For example, on April 18, 2008, a "Save the American Worker" rally was held outside El Sol. The rally was organized by a loose coalition of organizations opposed to unauthorized immigration. Among those who contributed to the event as speakers were Joyce Kaufman, a Fort Lauderdale–based radio talk-show host; Allen West, soon to be a controversial freshman member of the U.S. House of Representatives from Florida's Twenty-Second District; and Gayle Harrell, then a state House representative from another district who sponsored a bill that would have shut down centers such as El Sol.

Joyce Kaufman's radio show frequently focuses on the issue of illegal immigration, and El Sol is a prime target for her and her listeners. Kaufman was the target of a Federal Communications Commission (FCC) complaint for stating on her show, "If you commit a crime while you're here, we should hang you and send your body back to where you came from, and your family should pay for it." At the 2008 rally outside El Sol, Kaufman drew cheers from the crowd of fifty or sixty protesters as she exclaimed, "I'm tired [of hearing] teachers who have been forced to take a training on how to teach classes to children who don't speak the English language . . . it's an outrage! I live in a land where English is the language, and I'm tired of being embarrassed about that! I refuse to stand back as my laws, and my language, and my culture, and my borders disappear . . . it's an outrage!" Ironically, the loudspeakers and cheers were simultaneously disrupting three dozen migrant workers taking ESL classes upstairs at El Sol.

At the same rally, Allen West spoke at length about issues of national security and the expenditure of taxpayer dollars on "illegals." Speaking just feet from the doors of El Sol, West claimed that "the number one language being learned by Hezbollah Islamic terrorists right now is Spanish. . . . They're coming across our border . . . [and] if we don't get serious about securing our border, we're going to lose our country." West ended his speech by reminding the crowd to remain focused and active in the 2010 elections, and in light of the results the crowd was listening: in November 2010 West shocked observers when he handily unseated Democrat Ron Klein in Florida's Twenty-Second District. The week after the election he announced that radio shock jock Joyce Kaufman would serve as his chief of staff. Less than a week after the announcement, Kaufman stepped down from the position, citing concerns that her critics might use her to commit a "high-tech lynching" of Representative West.

Divisive immigration politics and rhetoric have infused state-level races in Florida as well. In November 2010 Rick Scott was also celebrating a victory in Florida's gubernatorial race and the election of a veto-proof majority in the Florida legislature. Scott ran as an outsider, emphasizing the immigration issue in his primary victory over Republican Bill McCollum. While McCollum initially voiced his disagreement with Arizona's controversial SB1070 immigration law in the primary campaign, he quickly changed tack and began working with state Representative William Snyder to introduce the first draft of a similar piece of legislation for Florida. The resulting Florida Immigration Enforcement Act would have been particularly onerous. As initially proposed, the act would have allowed law enforcement officers to accept passports as sufficient proof of legal residency from immigrants from Canada and European countries while requiring further documentation from other immigrants. In other words, it appeared to endorse explicit racial profiling. The bill also included language about the issue of day labor, including a provision that "it is unlawful for a person who is unlawfully present in the United States and who is an unauthorized alien to . . . solicit work in a public place or perform work as an employee or independent contractor in this state."[8] The bill ultimately failed to pass in the Florida Senate owing to pressure from the business sector, especially agriculture and tourism. The governor, however, continues to maintain his support for such legislation, and Florida lawmakers have closely monitored events in Alabama and Georgia, where state legislatures passed extremely restrictive immigration bills in 2011.

THE NATIONAL CONTEXT

Although immigration has long been a contentious issue in American politics, the controversy surrounding the opening of El Sol was magnified because it took place in the context of back-to-back failed attempts to enact national immigration reform laws in 2006 and 2007. With the stalemate in Washington, the situation was ripe for national anti-immigration groups like the Federation for American Immigration Reform (FAIR) to tap into local frustration.[9] In addition to further polarizing the debate, these organizations have contributed, through their campaigns, to the creation of a patchwork of local, state, and federal laws and ordinances designed to restrict or deflect unauthorized immigration. Across the United States, municipalities have imposed limits on access to services, passed ordinances against renting to or hiring unauthorized day laborers, and entered into collaborative agreements with federal immigration authorities such as the 287(g) agreements and the Secure Communities program.[10] For the most part, these tactics have done little to address the root causes or impact of unauthorized migration. Rather, they serve to polarize the debate about immigration and foster a growing climate of fear in immigrant communities across the country.

As both the George W. Bush and subsequently the Barack Obama administrations prepared to enter the immigration debate, each girded itself by ramping up immigration enforcement measures targeted primarily at the most vulnerable (and least politically powerful) group involved in the debate—individual unauthorized immigrants. Immigration and Customs Enforcement (ICE) removal rates jumped from just over 100,000 per year in 2001 and 2002 to nearly

350,000 in 2007 under the Bush administration. The Obama administration has continued this trend, with the number of removals reaching a total of nearly 400,000 per year in 2009, 2010, and 2011. While such efforts have split families and dashed hopes for a better future in many immigrant-sending communities in Mexico and Central America, their effectiveness in convincing the American people that either administration seriously wanted to produce a workable immigration policy remains in question. This toxic atmosphere produced a wave of local and state activism on immigration and sidetracked rational debate about immigration policy at the national level.

The themes and controversies swirling around immigration issues in general, and around El Sol in particular, represent a collision of local, national, and global forces. El Sol was founded as a local organization designed to address neighborhood quality-of-life issues, but it has come to represent much more to all sides engaged in the country's immigration debate. The push-and-pull factors that combined to fuel the growth of Jupiter's immigrant population in the first place are far beyond the control of local actors. In the face of rapid and unfamiliar change, all players in this drama have sought to control what they can—their own local environment. For those who oppose El Sol as part of a larger concern about immigration, this has taken the form of largely symbolic actions: protests, writing letters to representatives, and a push for further legislation to deflect or restrict immigration. As for the immigrants themselves, they have focused on internal organization—turning inward to seek mutual support—as well as on building links to other organizations and potential allies. For the elected politicians of Jupiter and their staffs, the process became their first tentative venture into making "social" policy at a municipal level.

THEMES AND ISSUES

In August 2001 Jupiter's town manager, Robert Bartolotta, convened an informal meeting to address the issues arising from Jupiter's growing immigrant community and the open-air day labor market. Members of the Jupiter Police Department; the neighborhood enhancement coordinator for the town; the principal of the local elementary school where the children of most of Jupiter's immigrants were enrolled; a representative of the MacArthur Foundation; Jerónimo Camposeco, a Mayan community leader and family support specialist with the Farmworker Child Development Center; and Dr. Timothy Steigenga, a professor of political science at the Jupiter campus of Florida Atlantic University (FAU), gathered in Bartolotta's conference room to talk about Jupiter's growing immigrant community. That 2001 meeting initiated a five-year process that would see Jupiter going against the tide of national immigration policy and culminate in the opening of El Sol. Most of the themes with which this book is concerned were evident at that initial meeting.

First, the questions arising in Jupiter represented the intersection of global and local factors. The forces that were causing Guatemalans to leave their homes in highland communities and come to a place like Jupiter were complicated and fundamentally misunderstood by most participants in the conversation. Camposeco, one of the oldest and best-established Mayan residents of Jupiter, explained the fact that many of Jupiter's immigrants had not come by choice but had been forced from their homes as refugees from Guatemala's civil war. He also pointed out that Jupiter's Guatemalan and Mexican communities were not primarily composed of Hispanics, as the town representatives had assumed, but were largely Mayan. Nor were they a single group that could be easily reached or communicated with via a single source, as they came from different villages in southern Mexico and Guatemala, spoke different indigenous languages (as well as Spanish), and had little in the way of formal organization.

Second, it quickly became clear that local quality-of-life issues were becoming intertwined with the national immigration debate in a manner that would not be easy to untangle. As the most visible element of the immigrant influx, day labor was quickly becoming a flashpoint for conflict in Jupiter. Native-born residents of the town were faced with a series of changes beyond their control, including demographic shifts, a red-hot real estate market, and neighborhoods where single-family homes were giving way to rental units. Although these changes had multiple causes, many residents focused on the one that was most visible and salient—the immigrants themselves. The police chief, the town manager, and the assistant town manager all became targets of pointed complaints and suggestions about what should be done about the growing immigrant community. Over time the tenor of resident complaints became increasingly shrill, as national and state-level anti-immigration groups inserted themselves into the local debate.

Third, the issues on the table in 2001 involved a complex set of human needs that did not fit neatly into traditional political categories. The residents' complaints were not initially infused with political or partisan rhetoric. For the most part, they were looking for solutions to the local quality-of-life problems associated with rapidly expanding and changing neighborhoods. In the early years, they were neither unified nor organized around national or even local immigration policy. Interestingly, the same could be said of the volunteers and supporters of the El Sol center today. More than a decade ago and today, the issue was and is framed by those closest to it primarily in human rather than political terms. The case of Jupiter suggests that one productive way forward on national immigration issues lies in the human relationships that have the power to reframe the debate, one individual and community at a time.

Finally, the 2001 meeting made it obvious that there was no existing vehicle for open exchange and positive collaboration between immigrants and town authorities. The immigrants themselves faced a series of significant problems, but they had no representation and few contacts within the town. Day laborers were often targets of muggings because many of them did not have bank accounts and carried their cash with them on payday. Camposeco explained that many were reluctant to report robberies for fear of interacting with the police. He also raised the issue of wage theft, pointing out that many day laborers worked at jobs for which they were never paid. Although the meeting represented a good start, there was no bridge between the immigrants and town authorities with which to continue the dialogue.

The 2001 meetings ultimately concluded with the somewhat vague consensus that the group would seek to raise awareness and understanding in the town about the diversity of the community and its new Hispanic and Mayan residents. All agreed that before we could proceed with further plans, a needs-assessment survey should be undertaken to glean further information about the local immigrant community. A group of student volunteers from the Wilkes Honors College of FAU was enlisted to help gather information from a sample of immigrants at an event sponsored at a local church.

In the chapters that follow, we recount the events that occurred since these initial steps of 2001, with a particular focus on the perspectives of neighborhood residents, local policy makers, representatives of the immigrant community, and advocates for the center. This book represents not only a retelling of the events and processes involved in establishing the center but also the stories of some of the many individuals and groups who came together to make it happen. Throughout the narrative, we include their stories, as well as commentary on the various themes and issues that arise along the way. It is our sincere hope that this book will be instructive for other communities facing similar issues.

GUIDE TO THE BOOK

We chose to organize the book in a primarily chronological fashion. The first chapter outlines the rapid changes that led to tensions in neighborhoods near the center of Jupiter, how the town reacted to those tensions, and the manner through which neighborhood issues came to be framed in terms of the larger immigration debate. Ironically, the town's early attempts to address quality-of-life issues through neighborhood programs fostered a process that mobilized neighborhood groups around immigration issues. In 2004 members of one of those groups invited representatives of FAIR to their meetings. From that point forward, the group coalesced under banner of the Jupiter Neighbors against Illegal Labor and framed neighborhood concerns in terms of immigration policy and law enforcement. Tensions in Jupiter rose to a crescendo in late 2004 and early 2005, as the Town Council debated the possibility of a resource center without yet taking any concrete action.

Without an understanding of the forces that drive migration, local authorities and citizens are likely to fundamentally misunderstand the people living in their communities, the circumstances that brought them there, and the policies that might best address the issues arising from their presence. Chapter 2 details the history of immigration to Jupiter in the context of the recent trend toward new destinations for Latino immigration. Jerónimo Camposeco, one of the earliest Guatemalans to settle in Jupiter, describes the chain of migration from Jupiter's sister city, Jacaltenango, Guatemala. As he explains, Jupiter's immigrants first organized to celebrate a religious and cultural ceremony, the Fiesta of Candelaria in 2001. Through these efforts they became, for the first time, a visible part of the Jupiter community as something other than day laborers. Organizing for the fiesta and connecting with the local university led to the creation of a pilot community and labor center initially operated by Corn Maya Inc.[11] As the immigrant community organized for their own purposes, they also began to gain access to town authorities for the first time, to form links with local churches and educational institutions, and develop relationships with non-immigrant residents.

Chapter 3 explores the Town Council debate surrounding the issue of day labor and the efforts to organize a community and labor center, the tensions that grew during the debate, and the coalition of forces that eventually emerged in support of El Sol. Here the roles of local leaders, electoral politics, media coverage, and negotiations with town authorities in the process of opening the center are explored. Since opening in September 2006, El Sol has evolved into a full-service immigrant integration center. Chapter 4 outlines the many programs that El Sol offers today and recounts the challenges, institutional growing pains, and successes that it has enjoyed in its first five years of operation. El Sol has successfully overcome many obstacles to become one of the most institutionalized and well-established nonprofit organizations in northern Palm Beach County. Its success, however, has also meant that it has become a magnet for anti-immigrant groups seeking to make a statement about immigration policy. Although the 2010 local elections marked the end of organized protests at El Sol, a group of approximately one dozen sign-waving protesters were a weekly Saturday fixture at the center for a number of years.

El Sol's mission is based on the assumption that true integration occurs when immigrants and the native born work together to achieve common goals and resolve local issues. In chapter 5, the story of one family whose lives have been fundamentally altered by El Sol highlights the role that the center plays in Jupiter as a place where immigrants and the native born can come together, get to know each other, and begin to build bridges of understanding.

The conclusion lays out the practical lessons to be gleaned from the El Sol experience. The chain of events in Jupiter suggests that many of the questions raised by those who oppose comprehensive immigration reform are already being addressed by forward-thinking local communities. Although many of them are unauthorized or have family members who are out of status, Jupiter's immigrants have become an integral and more integrated part of the community.

Finally, we should clarify a point about the sources for this work. In some cases the names of individuals have been changed in order to protect their identity. Over the course of this project, we guaranteed confidentiality to those who granted us interviews according to the Human Subjects Research Protocols of the University of Florida and Florida Atlantic University. Many of those we interviewed for this book chose to have their names included. Other interviews were conducted with public representatives who gave explicit permission for reproduction here. Statements from e-mails, letters, and other communications with Jupiter officials are part of the public record and are reproduced here, with a few exceptions, without names attached. For the most part, the events and processes described are from our own firsthand experience and are thus subject to all the bias and potential inaccuracies attendant upon such accounts.

From Back Burner to Center Stage

How Jupiter's Melting Pot Boiled Over

Pine Gardens North and South were very white, working-class
neighborhoods . . . that's how it was. That changed over time in ways that
government didn't even recognize at first. In some ways, shame on us.

—KAREN GOLONKA, Jupiter mayor

GROWING PAINS IN A COASTAL SOUTH FLORIDA COMMUNITY

On February 12, 2000, the town of Jupiter sponsored a party to celebrate its
seventy-fifth anniversary. Incorporated in 1925, Jupiter experienced a brief boom
period just before the Great Depression, but its population remained relatively
small in comparison with nearby Florida cities. At the time of the 1970 census,
Jupiter had 3,136 residents. By 1980 the population had more than tripled to
9,868, but Jupiter remained a very small town compared to the nearby city of
West Palm Beach (population 63,305 in 1980). It was not until 1987 that construction on Interstate 95 brought the expressway through the northern edge
of Palm Beach County and the town of Jupiter. Interstate 95 has since expanded
from six to ten lanes at the Jupiter exits. Like many cities in South Florida and
across the Southeast, Jupiter experienced growth and development at an unprecedented rate from the late 1980s through the late 2000s.

The MacArthur Foundation held large tracts of undeveloped land in northern Palm Beach County, including much of what today makes up Jupiter. In
the 1970s and 1980s the foundation began selling off relatively small parcels to
several developers, and by 1999 it had released most of its land. One developer
explained that "all of a sudden, when the MacArthur portfolio opened up, it
was like the California gold rush."[1] Upscale gated communities began appearing along the intercoastal waterway in Jupiter.

The sale of the MacArthur lands intensified the planning and construction
of upscale communities in Jupiter and surrounding areas. In 1999 Divosta began

developing Abacoa, a planned community containing multiple neighborhoods, commercial areas, an FAU campus, a stadium and spring training facility for the Florida Marlins and Saint Louis Cardinals, and an eighteen-hole golf course. By May 1999 Divosta was building at a pace of three structures daily to meet the demand generated by the rapid sales in Abacoa. In less than ten years, thousands of luxury homes were built and sold in Abacoa's nineteen residential neighborhoods. By the time Jupiter celebrated its seventy-fifth anniversary in 2000, the town had almost forty thousand residents, several golf courses, and multiple gated communities. The 2010 census put Jupiter's population at over fifty-five thousand residents.

In stark contrast to the mansions of Jupiter's gated communities and the luxury homes in Abacoa, the older neighborhoods in the center of town were built much earlier and consist of more modest single-story homes. These neighborhoods—Pine Gardens North, Pine Gardens South, Eastview Manor, Jupiter Plantation, and Jupiter River Estates especially—became the epicenter of the events that frame this story. As new structures rose all around Jupiter, new people were also moving in. The new residents of Jupiter included both the owners of the upscale homes in the new communities and the workers building and maintaining these expensive properties. Significant numbers of the new service and construction workers were immigrants from Guatemala and southern Mexico, who also began to settle in some of the city's older neighborhoods. Amid the hustle and bustle of the economic boom, these newcomers only gradually came to the attention of town administrators, as established residents, well-versed in neighborhood activism, began to voice concerns about changes taking place in Jupiter.

Town Manager Andy Lukasik had ten years of experience in the public sector, but he had never seen anything like the growth he witnessed in Jupiter: "Coming to Southeast Florida from Michigan it was insane. The landscape changed every single day. Every time you turned around, there was a new house being built, there was a new commercial plaza being built." As the new buildings went up, inexpensive labor was needed to maintain them. "We had the influx of folks coming from Guatemala," Lukasik recalled. "How it began, I don't know, but that's where we are now. They filled this need for labor at this time of unprecedented growth."

Jupiter's mayor, Karen Golonka, had a background in urban planning and development, but even for her the pace at which Jupiter was growing at the time was astounding. "We didn't have a lot of growth controls in place," she explained, "so it was all very political, constantly. Trying to get anything in place was hard."

Resident Mary Anne Oblaczynski grew up in Jupiter and the surrounding areas. As a longtime homeowner in Pine Gardens South in the center of town, she is in a unique position to speak to changes that have taken place in her neighborhood over the years and the economic and social forces that propelled those changes. In a brief interview conducted in 2011, Oblaczynski recalled some of the changes that came to her neighborhood during the years of rapid growth.

I moved to Pine Gardens South twenty-six years ago. At that time I had three children. Two years later my fourth one was born. I have raised my children there in Pine Gardens South. Twenty-six years ago Pine Gardens South was a mostly white neighborhood. If there were any [immigrants back then] they were a small minority. . . . We had one or two black families maybe. It was mostly white, working class. We started seeing the influx of the immigrant population. Right around fifteen years ago, it really started to ebb in. I did know that there was more of an immigrant population over by Center Street.

When Oblaczynski moved into the neighborhood in 1985, Pine Gardens South still lacked many basic amenities. In the years that followed, she and her neighbors began to organize and take advantage of new neighborhood improvement programs. "When I moved into Pine Gardens South," she recalled, "we had dirt streets. Our neighborhood, in the center of town, had dirt streets!" Getting the city to pave their streets required the neighbors to organize and voice their concerns as a group. This was their first major success. Yet there was still a lot of work to be done. Oblaczynski remembers their initial struggles to organize the neighborhood and work with the town in development projects.

Twenty-two or twenty-three years ago, a program called "communities in school" was going around. What they were trying to do was work with neighborhood schools and the neighborhoods they served—Jupiter Elementary and Pine Gardens South—to start developing programs, both to help within the schools but also to benefit the neighborhoods. In our neighborhood, we were doing programs, but we were not going anywhere. A core group of us, we kept having meetings and meetings and talking about what we wanted to see or do, but we were not really moving forward. It was a new thing for all of us. A core group of us stuck together and said, "OK, we need to do something, how do we go about it?" We knew that if we wanted to get any funds, or get anything, we had to form a 501(c)(3). To this day that is maintained, it is called Pine Gardens Community Organization, Inc. . . . Then the town did get the neighborhoods program, and this program was looking at some different ways and they came up with the Charter Neighborhoods thing. We almost didn't get to be the pilot because we were already organized. We fought, we argued for them to let us do it. They came around.

THE CHARTER NEIGHBORHOODS

The Charter Neighborhood program mentioned by Oblaczynski was designed to help neighborhoods help themselves through grants for infrastructural improvements (traffic calming, neighborhood beautification programs, etc.) and to engage residents in their own neighborhoods. Mayor Karen Golonka initially proposed the program and now sees it as the beginning of the town's engagement with the neighborhoods. Jupiter was beginning a major period of transition when Golonka took office, and the neighborhood enhancement program was something new. It took time to change the culture and mindset of council members and the community. As she explains: "Until the 1990s town government was very typical government: it wasn't that far-removed from really being a small-town government.[2] There was a change in the education and thought process of the council in some way. When I got onto the council, mostly the council members were blue collar, working class, and they may have had a little different perspective. They regarded government as the basic services. Maybe there just hadn't been any demand for anything else."

As the neighborhood programs began to get traction they did bring real changes to the "charter neighborhoods" in town. According to Town Manager Andy Lukasik, "The vast majority of the folks in the charter neighborhoods are predominantly lower middle income. There's a mixture of owner and rental occupied units . . . maybe an even split. There were pockets that were heavily rental units. A lot of the emphasis of the original charter neighborhoods program focused on infrastructure investment. You compare the older neighborhoods to Abacoa and you could see the infrastructure was starting to deteriorate."

Abacoa, with a planned downtown and amphitheater, New England–style architecture, and open green spaces, is almost the polar opposite of the small homes on numbered streets in Pine Gardens South in the center of "old Jupiter." Nonetheless, the red-hot real estate market that drove the construction of Abacoa and other communities in Jupiter impacted the entire town. According to Census and American Community Survey data, in 1990 there were only 14,602 housing units in Jupiter, with a median value of $108,400. By the year 2000 there were 21,054 units with a median value of $149,200. The median value of homes in Jupiter was up to $345,000 with a total of 26,040 units by 2005.

As Jupiter grew by leaps and bounds, the town looked for ways to engage the residents of its charter neighborhoods in quality-of-life improvement projects. To encourage people to organize on their own behalf, town administrators sent residents to seminars and conferences on neighborhood development. At these events participants learned how to build social networks and approach elected officials. As Andy Lukasik later recalled, "The strategies that they were learning—that we were trying to empower them with—they used these strategies quite effectively to get attention about the quality-of-life issues that they were experiencing."

As the town worked with residents in the charter neighborhoods to make local improvements and train leaders in organizing and articulating their concerns to local government, some of the early concerns about quality-of-life issues began to emerge more prominently. But at this point, according to Lukasik, the concerns were rarely couched in terms of immigration.

You would see laced throughout some of these strategic plans that the neighborhoods put together some references about the impacts that the rental units were having. I didn't necessarily read it that way when I started paging through the plans, but you did see things about overcrowding, littering, and things of that nature. People didn't necessarily associate it with immigration, but some of those things were wrapped into the initial plans. They would get pointed to frequently as we started seeing the intensity of the debate and the cries about the impact of the day labor phenomenon on the neighborhoods being articulated to our council members. . . . Our efforts to empower residents within our neighborhoods, to learn how to mobilize and come to council and ask for things that they really needed . . . that really was the foundation for it. When people started showing up at council meetings, they started showing up dressed in red. Well, that was a tactic that they learned from some of the seminars that we brought them to. They figured out that tactic from us! They used the strategies that they learned from us to start getting attention.

Town Council member Jim Kuretski agreed: "Interestingly, the issue of immigration was only hot in the charter neighborhoods. In a way we created some of this heat. We had empowered the neighborhoods to convene, create a vision statement, and work toward achieving that. We enabled, in a way, some of the mobilization that happened. We gave them the avenues."

Neighborhoods built in part on the activism of older residents began to draw a diverse set of newcomers, nonimmigrants as well as immigrants. As Oblaczynski recalls: "People were looking for neighborhoods. Some of the middle-class folks that came with the boom were the ones who felt most affected. My neighborhood is a great place for young families. You have the elementary school within walking distance, the library, a beautiful park. It's in the center of town. You have all the amenities, great athletic programs. It is a great place for an up-and-coming family to buy in, to move in. You have a nice neighborhood where your kids can all play. That's exactly where the families of the immigrants looked, too, and said, 'Wow, this is nice.'"

Frequently, antipathy toward immigrants is associated with economic downturns. Yet, as events in Jupiter show, uneasiness can arise even in the midst of unprecedented growth and expansion. Oblaczynski articulates a common dynamic.

> We also started seeing an influx of the immigrants. There was a little bit of a clash. Some were like, "Wait a minute, I moved into this neighborhood because it was nice, white middle class. . . . What are you doing here, and why are fifteen of your family members with you?" That was the attitude. It was the perception that people had that their comfort zone was being threatened. . . . They had in their mind what their lifestyle and their neighborhood should be. No, we don't have the picket fences, but that's what they were seeing and looking for, the Ozzie and Harriet neighborhood. They moved into these neighborhoods as "This is my starter house. I will live here for a while and eventually will move." I think there was a threat. The comfort zone got taken away. The people whose comfort zone was very threatened were looking at it economically and socially. "Do I want my kids hanging out with people who might not be here legally?"

Neighborhood Complaints and Muted Responses

As the neighborhoods changed, a series of related issues and complaints were raised by residents and brought to the attention of the Town Council and the town manager's office. Although the issues frequently overlapped, the primary complaints had to do with overcrowding, public drunkenness, public urination, trash and littering, loitering and trespassing (along Center Street's informal day labor pickup location), traffic issues, intimidating behavior toward women, reduced property values, and crime. The venue for many of these complaints was the very neighborhood enhancement programs the town had encouraged and supported in the neighborhoods. Minutes from the December 2002 Town Council meetings show residents asking the town to do something about the day labor situation on Center Street, citing safety concerns, depreciation of property values (despite the fact that property values were in fact increasing at the time), and trespassing.

The Town Council heard continuing complaints throughout 2003, with increasing numbers of residents citing the Center Street day labor market as the locus of the problems. Residents also began contacting town officials directly to voice their concerns. In a 2003 e-mail to the town, a resident of Center Street explained his grievances: "Every morning there is a large amount of migrant workers on the south side of Center Street waiting for contractors to pick them up for work. This is a residential area and should not be used for a gathering

Day laborers crowding around a pickup truck in front of the apartments on Center Street prior to the opening of El Sol (Courtesy of Sister Marta Tobón)

place to seek employment." In a direct letter to the mayor the same year, he expressed his growing frustration with the lack of action on the part of the town.

> On Sunday, October 13, 2003, the noise emanating from the apartments on Center Street and Pennock lane was unbearable. It was the equivalent to living next to an airport. I am referring to the Guatemalans who rent apartments opposite of Jupiter Plantation [a neighborhood adjacent to Center Street]. . . . Besides the loud music, these people are congregating every morning waiting for rides and are blocking the sidewalk. It has become a hazardous situation for motorists and pedestrians. Please see what you can do to remedy this deplorable situation. I have lived in Jupiter for 23 years and have never witnessed a situation like this. It is totally unacceptable and will inevitably devaluate property values in and around our area. This situation is noticeably escalating. Those who are not chosen to work are not dispersing and going back to their apartments, but continue to loll around the sidewalks, sitting on the curbs and laying down on the grass and sleeping there. It is more suitable a view as would be seen in Mexico, Guatemala or other Central American countries. These persons are clearly loitering and running down the neighborhood. What is amazing is that this condition has been prevalent for many months in spite of the fact that there have been many complaints to this prevailing situation.

At the request of the mayor, the Jupiter Police Department had issued a report in early 2003 detailing the "Center Street Problems." According to this report, the department had responded to 355 calls for service in the Center Street area. The police had tried several methods to resolve the issues. They had placed "No Trespassing" signs in several key locations and called the Immigration and Naturalization Service. The report from the Police Department reads, "INS was contacted due to many of the subjects in question being illegal immigrants. We received a positive reply from INS at first, but since 9/11 we have been advised they do not have the manpower to assist us. Apparently the response from INS to Guatemalan illegal aliens is different to that of others." The Police Department sought to relocate the workers to a place where they would not be a nuisance to other town residents, but these efforts were also futile. Officers then encouraged the workers to get identification cards so that they could seek jobs through a local hiring agency, but "due to the illegal immigration status of most, they did not take advantage of this solution." When the police contacted a local Baptist church to ask if the day laborers might use the parking lot there to await jobs, church officials denied the request for liability reasons.

Clearly frustrated, Jupiter's chief of police concluded his report with an assessment that captures the principal dilemma faced by local law enforcement in communities that seek to address the complex issues raised by immigration based solely on local enforcement methods: "The Police Department's problem, as a law enforcement agency, is the numerous calls we receive from citizens who are upset with the presence of Guatemalans and Mexicans that stand along the sidewalks on Center Street waiting to be selected for employment. On the other hand we receive complaints from the citizens in the community and the workers themselves that we (Police) are harassing them and making it difficult for them to get work. It does seem at times it is a no win situation for us, but that doesn't stop us from trying to find an amicable solution."

As the police were exploring their own methods of dealing with the growing neighborhood problems, members of the town staff were conducting research on a housing ordinance under consideration, the possibility of moving the hiring site to an industrial area, and potential immigration and code enforcement measures to address the Center Street complaints. For the most part, however, elected representatives listened to the complaints during this period (2001–3) but made little public comment and took no immediate action. Although the staff was engaged in research and developing alternatives for dealing with the quality-of-life issues, the Town Council was not prepared to invest funds or resources in the issue at this early juncture.

Talking with Mayor Golonka, council member Kuretski, and (at that time) Assistant Town Manager Lukasik about this period sheds significant light on the town's initial lack of response. For his part, Andy Lukasik initially felt that in the context of the many issues the town was dealing with, the Center Street complaints were not a top priority in 2001 and 2002. Furthermore, it was hard to take some of the early complaints seriously. As Lukasik recalls: " I probably received a couple of phone calls about it: people standing on the sidewalk, soliciting for jobs. Frankly, I didn't pay much attention. I knew they were Hispanic, maybe some of them weren't here legally. I wrote it all off as, 'Well, it's racism, it's reactionary. This is really a nonsensical complaint. We shouldn't even be paying attention to this.' And quite frankly, I did not pay attention to a lot of those early complaints."

But Lukasik's initial reaction soon changed, as he became one of the first people associated with the town to begin to think seriously about solutions to the Center Street problems. Later in 2002 he began to see the neighborhood issues in a more serious light. He quickly began to see the larger picture surrounding day labor and the potential for escalating tensions in Jupiter.

> I realized this could be a bigger problem than I ever thought. I had no understanding of the dynamics or the impact on the community. I had no understanding of anything relating to undocumented migration. It never came into play in my daily life until you [Steigenga] and I started talking about it. Then I had a better understanding of things, where the immigrants were coming from, why they were here, and what the potential impact could be. You enlightened me to the whole day labor phenomena—the things that happen in a community when you have the convergence of an immigrant population in an area that perhaps isn't ready for it. All the things, starting with the labor, the demand for the labor, the solicitation, the hanging out on the street, the fear that it starts putting into people who drive by and live in the neighborhood. It may have been unfounded in some cases, but the fear is real nonetheless. There are also secondary impacts of standing around: the traffic, the litter, debris, public urination. There are impacts day labor has on individuals themselves: standing in the sun, the rain, and the cold all day. What started becoming more evident and what started raising the issue at Town Council was the ultimate impact in the neighborhoods: the overcrowding, the impacts of overcrowding, the noise, the litter, the cultural issues, the drinking. All those things started boiling up in the neighborhoods, and that's when the council started realizing that we had an issue.

Although Lukasik's perspective on what the town could do about the situation quickly evolved, he remained constrained by the larger political process and the manner in which the Town Council was approaching the issue—or failing to approach it. At that time the council was still limiting itself to planning and building the infrastructure needed in a community undergoing rapid growth. In those days, he explains, "local government didn't really have much to do with social issues."

Interviews with Town Council members, especially those who would come to be supporters of the El Sol Neighborhood Resource Center, confirm Lukasik's diagnosis of the early paralysis on the part of the council. Jim Kuretski recalls:

> I'm not exaggerating, but in 2001 I had no clue we had any immigration in this town. Maybe the second year I heard you were around. I thought,

"Gee, that's kind of nice that we have this professor in town who is kind of working with the immigrants." I thought maybe we had a few immigrants. I lived by Loxahatchee Road and we would see them on Center Street. Most people get up in the morning, go to work, come home . . . [and] they don't really pay attention to what is going on around them. I am as guilty of that as anybody. It was amazing when I finally realized that there was an immigrant population. I am not exaggerating. . . . One day I thought, "Gee, there's an immigrant issue!" I was flabbergasted by how many immigrants I was seeing! They were there, and I just wasn't seeing them before. I would drive to and from work, I worked in Juno Beach, and I was literally counting now. How could I have missed that?! They were really all in the shadows!

Once he became aware of the issue, it still took Councilman Kuretski some time to become convinced that local government should play a role in managing it. A fiscal conservative trained as an engineer, Kuretski initially believed that it was an issue for the federal government.

While Kuretski would go on to become an outspoken advocate for El Sol, the mayor remained on the fence about the issue for some time. Although she eventually voted to support opening El Sol, she also explains her initial reluctance to engage the issue as a town representative: "It was a new type of problem. I think to some extent we kind of hoped it would just go away. Initially it was a police and code issue when it hadn't really raised so much to the council level on a continuous basis. Our first reaction, particularly about people hanging around on the street, was why can't we just stop it?" Faced with complaints from residents, the mayor explained that the police had called the INS and there was not much local government could do. As she explains, "We probably were just hoping that somehow things would just work themselves out. Unless there is somebody who really steps forward to be an advocate then government kind of lets things ride until it reaches the point where something has to be done about it."

Forging Bonds and Building Bridges

As established residents began to organize, immigrants, too, were starting to find their voice. In early 2002 representatives of Corn Maya Inc. approached the town to ask for access to soccer fields for the immigrant community. As outlined in the next chapter, Corn Maya emerged as a formal nonprofit representing the immigrant community in 2001 and 2002. Although Jupiter has many soccer fields, they are generally reserved for youth league soccer tournaments. Town authorities and immigrant soccer players engaged in a perpetual game of cat and mouse when the fields were not in use on weekends, the town wanting to keep the fields pristine for the next set of youth league games while the immigrants sought to use them for pickup soccer games. Ultimately the town's manager of parks and recreation made a field available on Sundays for the Guatemalan soccer leagues (utilizing local public school fields). Although this was a small step, it was a particularly important one. For the first time Jupiter's immigrant community had articulated a concern to local government and negotiated a favorable outcome.

At this point Andy Lukasik and members of his staff were beginning to do their own research and were coming to the conclusion that a resource center might help to resolve some of the neighborhood and day labor issues in Jupiter.[3] In meetings with town staff and representatives of the immigrant community, Lukasik encouraged Corn Maya to seek grant funding to open a pilot labor center. Corn Maya applied for and received a small grant from the Community Foundation for Palm Beach and Martin Counties in 2002 and opened an office near Center Street. Meanwhile Lukasik began speaking to council members about the possibility of a bigger center as part of a larger strategy for tackling neighborhood issues.

A third critical development was under way at Saint Peter, the Catholic Church in Jupiter, whose priest had recently taken a position elsewhere. Father Don Finney had worked with the diocese's Hispanic Ministry both in Palm Beach Gardens and north of Jupiter in Martin County. But he had never had his own church before. Aware of Jupiter's growing community of immigrants, he applied for the position. With a congregation of twenty-five hundred families that was growing by leaps and bounds, it was a big assignment—one that would place Father Finney and Saint Peter immediately into the center of the debate surrounding Jupiter's immigrant community.

As Father Finney soon discovered, there was a large demand for Spanish services in Jupiter that had long been unmet.

> Within the first couple of weeks there, I met with some of the Guatemalan leaders that had been going to Saint Ignatius. I said to them that I wanted to start a Spanish mass here and to get things going. It started very quickly— training ushers and lectors and Eucharistic ministries to give them the theology behind it. We would have the trainings here in the evenings. I was hoping maybe 10 people would show up, but 40–50 people showed up to

each of these trainings! One of the original plans was to have the mass on Sunday afternoons at 12:30 in the chapel. The chapel accommodates 250 people. We were planning for our first mass: all the liturgical ministers were trained . . . [and] some of them went door to door to hand out flyers announcing that at the end of May we would have the first Spanish-language mass at Saint Peter. So we had it in the church . . . and over 1,000 people were there on that first Sunday!

Soon Father Finney was joined at Saint Peter by three nuns, members of the Guadalupan Missionaries of the Holy Spirit. Among them was Sister Marta Tobón, who would come to play a major role in the development of El Sol. Sister Marta explained her introduction to the community.

> They asked us to come, and I said, "Yes, I am ready." They asked us to come around April. Father Don was new here—all of us, everything was new. The first thing that they showed us was Center Street. They were packed! We started here on August 1, 2003. That is how we started working. Then we started going to Center Street. We started with Sunday masses. . . . That is how we do our ministry. Our congregation focuses on evangelization and catechesis. We like being with the people . . . meeting them where they are. We do a lot of home visiting. We try to listen to them. We started out in the streets. The sisters went to their houses; we went and walked around Center Street trying to get to know them: who they were, what was happening to them.

The arrival of Sister Marta and Father Finney at Saint Peter had an immediate impact on Jupiter's immigrant community. For the first time, large numbers of Guatemalan and Mexican immigrants felt welcome in a local institution. There was space for meetings and access to information and institutional resources that had previously been absent. As detailed in the next chapter, Saint Peter would become the venue for meetings of the coalition of groups backing the creation of a neighborhood resource center.

So as of late 2003, Jupiter's immigrant community was beginning to find a voice and institutional support through Corn Maya and Saint Peter. At the same time, Jupiter's elected officials continued their hands-off approach to neighborhood complaints related to immigration. When e-mails with complaints about Center Street appeared, the town responded by saying that a pilot hiring center was being operated by a group of immigrants organized under Corn Maya, but

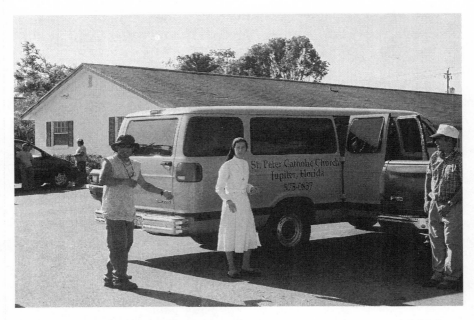

Sister Marta Tobón doing outreach along Center Street prior to the opening of El Sol
(Courtesy of El Sol, Jupiter's Neighborhood Resource Center)

that the size of the location limited its ability to fully resolve the Center Street
issues. Increasingly, all the stakeholders—neighborhood residents, immigrant
leaders, businesspeople, landlords, and others—began to express their frustration in ever more strident terms.

2004: The Year the Pot Began to Boil

Leading up to 2004, the town of Jupiter had done little to address the quality-
of-life complaints that residents of the charter neighborhoods had brought up.
Behind the scenes, however, town staff, spearheaded by Andy Lukasik, had
been researching the issues and meeting with representatives of the immigrant
community. In a Town Council meeting in early February 2004, Town staff
proposed a housing ordinance that would implement health and safety standards by limiting the number of people who were allowed to live in a unit,
depending on the unit size. Adopting the housing ordinance was among the
first official steps that the town of Jupiter took to address residents' complaints.
Town staff hoped that a housing ordinance to address the overcrowding problems would also have a positive effect on the other neighborhood issues. Unlike

measures taken in some other parts of the country, Jupiter's ordinance did not require residents to supply Social Security numbers. As Andy Lukasik explains:

> Our ordinance is based upon capacity. We looked at the impact on the neighborhoods, and we saw that there was a problem with capacity. The neighborhoods could not sustain what was going on. There were just too many people. That's why we were getting the littering, the urination, that's why we were getting all those things. There were cultural issues that we tried to address through education, but still a lot of life had to take place outside because there was no room inside! That pushed a lot of the nuisance issues out in public. So we took the next logical step: if there are too many people in these structures, then that's what we were going to go after. We did it strictly based on capacity; we didn't do it based upon whether or not people had documentation. We were not interested in that. We were interested in health and human safety.

By passing this ordinance, the town had recognized part of the problem and done something to address it. The ordinance served to put the more comprehensive set of neighborhood issues more firmly on the council's radar, a small but important victory for the town staff, which had been working on it for a long time behind the scenes. As an "enforcement" move, the passing of the ordinance laid a foundation of political capital on which more sophisticated and comprehensive solutions could be built.

For many residents of Jupiter, however, progress on the issues was still painfully slow. Tired of having her complaints fall on deaf ears at the town level, in January 2005 a Center Street resident wrote a letter to her county commissioner stating: "In the Town of Jupiter Florida we have a very bad and growing illegal alien problem—which I have to point out you have been silent and not interested in. Our Mayor, Town council, local Police, Code enforcement have been *very negligent* in addressing the issues. We all, on Center Street, have been very patient and way too tolerant while the Mayor et al. do nothing but talk and push us very concerned citizens aside. The Town does not enforce its own laws or that of the Federal Government!"

An article in the *Palm Beach Post* in February 2004 titled "Suburbanites, Day Laborers at Odds in Jupiter" also featured residents who explained their concerns with overcrowding, perceived decreasing property values, and other quality-of-life issues. As one resident put it, "They seem like nice people, the men waiting there, and we don't have any crime problem or anything like that. . . .

But my kids don't ride their bikes on Center Street anymore, and they don't take the school bus. There are so many of those men, and it's dark when the bus comes in the morning. It's too scary." Another resident cited in the article laments, "I hear they're very good workers, but that scene can't be helping our property values."[4]

Tensions over Center Street and the charter neighborhoods played only a minor role in the 2004 elections in Jupiter. The mayor and several council members were up for reelection in March. Councilwoman Babs Henderson gave up her seat on the Town Council to run for mayor against Karen Golonka. In an article in the *Palm Beach Post* during the run-up to the elections, Henderson alluded to the mayor and the council's inaction regarding the issues on Center Street. She also frequently criticized the council for not doing enough to deal with "illegal aliens" in her speeches. In the end, however, Golonka handily defeated Henderson and was reelected. Jim Kuretski also retained his seat, and Todd Woodraska was elected to the seat that Babs Henderson had given up to run against Golonka. At this point, in early 2004, development and growth continued to be the primary issues for Jupiter voters. Although Karen Golonka, Jim Kuretski, and Todd Woodraska all eventually were swayed to support the idea of a resource center to deal with the Center Street problem, the issue was still not front and center for them in the 2004 election campaign.

ONE STEP FORWARD AND TWO STEPS BACK

The newly elected Town Council met for the first time on April 6, 2004. Although the Center Street issue was not at the top of the agenda during the campaign season, it began bubbling up again during this first meeting following the elections. When the time came for citizens' comments, several people brought up the Center Street issues. Concerned neighbors appeared at this meeting with photographs of overflowing dumpsters and men standing around waiting for work on Center Street. The mayor acknowledged that the town had begun looking into the idea of relocating the workers but was doing nothing more concrete. Town Manager Robert Barlotta indicated that his staff was looking at six potential sites for relocation and had met with representatives from some of the sites. He also noted that his staff was preparing a report for the council to be presented in the coming weeks.

April 20, 2004, was a busy day for town government in Jupiter. Robert Barlotta had stepped down from his position as town manager, and Andy Lukasik was appointed as his successor. On the same day, Guatemalan vice president Eduardo Stein made a planned visit to South Florida with a stop in Jupiter.

More than three hundred members of the Guatemalan community gathered in the town's community center to hear him speak and to ask questions. At the event, Mayor Golonka presented Vice President Stein with a painting of the local lighthouse and a symbolic key to the city. He also met with representatives of Corn Maya.

While the meeting between the Guatemalan vice president and the mayor of Jupiter may have been symbolic, it was important because it further emphasized the growing importance of the issue of immigrants in Jupiter and gave a public face to the immigrant community. Coverage in the *Palm Beach Post* the next day noted that the immigrants had asked Stein to continue lobbying in Washington for immigration reform. The article also quoted the new town manager, Andy Lukasik, as stating that "progress is being made toward finding a site for a new labor center where employers can find laborers and that will get job seekers off Center Street."[5]

Despite the "feel-good" nature of the public event, the April 20 Town Council meeting was contentious once again. While the mayor and town manager were delayed at the event for the Guatemalan vice president, concerned neighborhood residents again showed up ready to be heard. At this Town Council meeting there were nine citizen comments, and all of them dealt directly with the issues on Center Street. One resident stated that there was a "strong element of crime" in his neighborhood and implored the council to take action: "Before we have a rape or murder, the INS should document these migrant workers, issue them green cards and deport illegals. Let's not wait before something more serious happens to take action. I am sure that city council members would not want that on their conscience, that they had done nothing to correct this dangerous situation."

Another resident stated that "people were laying on the sidewalk all day" along Center Street. Overcrowding, broken beer bottles, loud vehicles, and other nuisance complaints were also cited, and the council was exhorted to call the INS. Councilman Don Daniels ended the meeting by pointing out that he was upset with both the contractors and the "illegal workers" profiting while the neighborhood, town, and local businesses were paying the cost. He noted the need for an immediate resolution.

The issue of the labor center was raised again at the Town Council's May 25 workshop on the Community Investment Plan. By this point, Council member Kuretski was calling for immediate action. He noted that the town had invested in previous public-private partnerships and that the purchase of a building to serve as a day labor center could be a good investment for the town. The mayor, however, stated that the council needed more discussion before making any decisions and that more code enforcement strategies should be investigated before proceeding. The council ultimately placed two hundred thousand dollars in the five-year Community Investment Program (CIP) to resolve issues surrounding the open-air immigrant labor market on Center Street, but it made no specific recommendation as to how or when the money was to be spent.

While Andy Lukasik and his staff ultimately hoped to relocate the workers to an organized hiring site, the Town Council was not yet ready, politically, to make that call in the summer of 2004. As Lukasik explains, the council could agree on the enforcement piece, but the larger picture goals required more political support.

> We did have the enforcement piece to everything. Unfortunately because of the politics that's always where we had to start. We had to start with enforcement. We did zero tolerance on the things that were the most visible and had the greatest impact on quality of life in the neighborhoods. It really all started with a pragmatic approach to addressing quality-of-life issues. We knew that the center was going to be ultimately the centerpiece. We knew that it was going to be the key to help us be successful. We didn't know how it was going to work, but we knew that it had to be there. We also knew that politically it wasn't going to happen right away. We still built around it, knowing that ultimately the center was going to come. We didn't have the political support at the time. We had to at least get at some of the enforcement pieces: we had the overcrowding issues, the junk vehicles, the garbage always sitting out. . . . We went after all of those quality-of-life and human safety issues, the big ones that have a very large impact visually and just over general quality of life in the neighborhoods. That was going to be our charge.

At this point in the process, advocates for the creation of a center were beginning to believe they were on the verge of a breakthrough. The Town Council put the issue of a resource center on the agenda for a June 1 roundtable discussion. Representatives of Saint Peter Catholic Church, Corn Maya, and People Engaged in Active Community Efforts (PEACE) prepared a report on various potential sites in town that could serve as a center. At this same discussion, newly appointed Assistant Town Manager Robert Lecky began by noting that town employees had been conducting research on the issue since 2001 and were now requesting specific direction from the council. Lecky presented case studies from other communities dealing with day labor and quality-of-life issues and reviewed potential sites for a labor center in Jupiter. Among the options discussed at the meeting was an outdoor facility (like a bus station) near the train tracks. At this meeting Councilman Kuretski again noted that the Community Investment Program had become his number-one priority. He suggested that the town needed to take immediate action and supported the purchase of a building along Center Street, a building with a price tag near one million dollars.

Although this issue is covered in greater depth in the next chapter, it is worth pointing out that a grassroots lobbying process was ongoing throughout this period. The groups mentioned above met monthly at Saint Peter church to discuss the future of a resource center, produce background information, and assist staff with research on best practices in other communities. They also organized an informational meeting, which brought together more than one hundred individuals from the immigrant community, to do outreach and education about the housing ordinance and the proposed labor center. While many of the immigrant leaders were understandably nervous about the housing regulations, the idea of a center was looked upon favorably. At the same time, Corn Maya's small office on Old Dixie Highway in Jupiter served as a pilot labor and outreach center for the immigrant community. Although funding was scarce, Corn Maya continued to apply for grants and seek funding for a labor center that could be operated on town-owned property.

While the press had paid some attention to the Center Street and neighborhood issues in Jupiter, the idea of the town spending a million dollars on a building for a labor center immediately began to attract media attention. A June 6 article in the *Jupiter Courier* noted that the Town Council was considering the purchase of a parcel of land just south of Center Street for the development of a labor center. According to the paper, the property was valued at about nine hundred thousand dollars and the center would carry annual operating costs of approximately forty thousand.[6] On June 9 it ran an editorial in opposition to the Center. Public debate over the center was beginning to seriously heat up. In a July e-mail to the Town Council, an upset Center Street resident stated, "The time has come to take legal actions. I ask all members of the Council: are you willing to help these money-hungry contractors to line their pockets with illegal cash, or are you going to stand with the tax-paying, law-abiding citizens of Jupiter's blighted communities currently invaded by these illegal aliens and those who would exploit them?"

A second special Town Council workshop on Center Street and the neighborhoods was held in October 2004. At this workshop town employees again presented their findings on how other cities had dealt with similar issues and how other labor centers around the country were operating. One of the main issues discussed during this workshop was the location of a potential hiring site, as there were several being discussed. Each site posed different challenges (including cost, location, condition of the building, availability, and size), and they were discussed at large by the council. While no consensus was reached on a site or the level of involvement with such a project the town was willing to have, the council made it clear that it understood that something had to be done about the labor issue, and that the labor center idea was firmly on the table.

In December 2004 Town Manager Andy Lukasik sent a memorandum to the Town Council, outlining the "mitigation strategies" that he and an interdepartmental team had decided were to be implemented as soon as possible. The strategies included strict enforcement of the housing ordinance, the removal of "bad guys" from the neighborhoods with the assistance of the Police Department, outreach efforts conducted through a Hispanic neighborhood liaison, the opening of a resource center "recognizing the economic factors creating the neighborhood issues and providing employment opportunities/services to individuals residing in Jupiter," and finally a no-solicitation ordinance that would ban streetside solicitation for work in Jupiter. From the perspective of town staff all of these were necessary steps to clean up the appearance of the affected neighborhoods, build political capital, build trust within the immigrant community, and ultimately open a labor center.

After the town's two workshops focused on Center Street, the efforts of town staff, the housing ordinance, and the subsequent press coverage, the idea of a labor center began to gain notoriety in Jupiter. Both positive and negative correspondence began to pour in. Much like the Town Council at this point, the residents of Center Street were divided on the issue of a town-supported center. Some Center Street residents welcomed the idea because they saw it as a way to solve the neighborhood issues that had mobilized them in the first place. Others, however, opposed the idea of the center altogether and felt that the main issue was no longer neighborhood quality-of-life issues and was instead a broader problem of unauthorized immigration. Though a distinct minority, the latter group grew increasingly vocal and strident at Town Council meetings and via the local media.

Alien Forces in Jupiter

Those opposed to the center began to truly turn up the heat in Jupiter beginning in November 2004. Almost overnight neighborhood issues that were at the root of the original complaints took on a new tone—with complaints centered on immigration issues. In a November 15 e-mail to Mayor Karen Golonka, a resident of Jupiter Plantation (a community directly across from the day labor pickup area on Center Street) warned the town of the outside influences at play.

> During the past month a new group has appeared with an agenda concerning the workers on Center Street. This group's agenda is to try to intimidate you into not leasing or buying a hiring hall for the workers. Their tactics will be threats of legal action, etc. As you are all aware, the towns that have used hiring halls have never been successfully sued by anyone. I deeply regret this group, whose anti-immigrant slogans and ideas border on hysteria and might delay your decision regarding the hiring center. As you recall, Mayor Golonka, the meetings held over the past two years always spoke of a multi-pronged solution to the Center Street problem. The first [step] was the housing ordinance, which is now accomplished. The second was to be the hiring hall and the hall is also the social service center for the workers and their families. I am pleading with you all. There are many of us in Jupiter who have worked long and hard to reach a solution. We also believe that the workers are residents of Jupiter and are here to stay. If there are problems with their legality, that is up to the Federal Government and the INS to reconcile. As a retired educator here in town, I am deeply saddened that an outside organization (with many different agendas) may assist in delaying your decision about the hiring center.

The resident's letter refers to the appearance of the Federation for American Immigration Reform (FAIR) on the Jupiter scene. John Slattery (the leader of the group of Jupiter residents opposed to the idea of a labor center) and a few other residents of the charter neighborhoods contacted FAIR in 2004 when the Town Council began to have more serious discussions about opening a resource center.[7] The primary policy goal of FAIR is to reduce overall immigration levels in the United States, and the organization aggressively seeks allies in communities experiencing tensions like Jupiter's. The Southern Poverty Law Center has labeled FAIR a "hate group" and has reported that several of FAIR's key officials have long-standing ties to white supremacist and eugenics organizations. As the Jupiter Plantation resident had warned, on November 15 Michael Hethmon, an attorney from FAIR, sent a letter to Jupiter's mayor, threatening legal action against the town if it proceeded in support of the center. On its website, FAIR publishes information about "How Day Labor Hiring Sites Promote

Illegal Immigration" and details how communities should go about "Confronting Illegal Day Labor Issues."[8] In these documents, FAIR describes the day labor
pickup site issue as follows: "Typically, these sites will raise quality of life concerns, such as public safety, health, and welfare, as well as facilitating widespread
violations of immigration, employment, wage, health and safety, and tax laws."

While the first part of the FAIR statement accurately describes the initial concerns of Center Street residents in Jupiter, the issues of violations of immigration, employment, wage, and tax laws were not a prevalent part of community
complaints until FAIR made its appearance on the scene. After the November
2004 meeting with FAIR at Jupiter Plantation, there was a clear shift in the
rhetoric and tactics utilized by Jupiter residents concerned about the changes
in their neighborhoods. After years of inaction on the part of the council and
the now imminent possibility of a labor center as part of a proposed solution,
residents now began to articulate complaints in terms of an immigration policy
framework rather than a framework of neighborhood issues and quality of life.

One of the key tactics advocated by FAIR on its website and in its publications
is to persuade local activists to join or start a group to oppose immigrants in
the local community and promote federal immigration policy issues. In November 2004 a group of Jupiter residents opposed to the idea of a labor center formed
Jupiter Neighbors against Illegal Labor (JNAIL). According to its articles of
incorporation, the purpose of JNAIL was to engage in "political action to support politicians who are against the hiring of or building a labor hall for, the
illegal immigrants along Center Street in Jupiter, Florida." It is clear that for the
Jupiter residents who joined JNAIL, the issue had become more about unauthorized immigrants and immigration policy than about overcrowded apartments and disorderly streets. Members of JNAIL wearing red shirts showed up
at the November 16 Town Council meeting where tensions continued to rise
as those who spoke against the center encouraged the council to "send the illegal immigrants home."

Up to this point, news coverage about a labor center had remained primarily
local, but after the appearance of FAIR, the television network CNN contacted
local officials about doing a report on the labor center. On November 18 a segment on the Center Street issue aired on the nationally televised *Lou Dobbs
Tonight*. The segment opened with Lou Dobbs noting, "The absence of a clear
federal immigration policy is forcing many local communities to find ways to
deal with the invasion of illegal aliens. One Florida town is considering a plan
that would use outrageous amounts of taxpayer money to find a solution to its
problems." From there the scene changed to a shot of workers on Center Street

as the announcer stated, "Hundreds of workers line Center Street every morning in Jupiter, Florida, willing, ready, and illegal." Throughout the brief broadcast, the term *illegal* was emphasized by Dobbs, the reporter on site, and by all of the concerned residents interviewed for the piece.

On November 30 JNAIL held a second meeting with FAIR representatives at the Jupiter Plantation clubhouse. In attendance at this meeting were residents from all the charter neighborhoods (Jupiter Plantation, Pine Gardens North, Pine Gardens South, and Eastview Manor). Vice Mayor Don Daniels was also in attendance and addressed the crowd. The main speaker at the event, however, was an attorney from FAIR who had flown in from New York. The group decided at that meeting that its members would attend the next Town Council meeting en masse. Following this JNAIL meeting, they distributed flyers throughout the neighborhood to encourage attendance. By this point the original complaints related to quality-of-life issues in the neighborhoods had completely taken a backseat to wider immigration policy issues. The first page of the JNAIL flyer was focused on neighborhood issues and read, in part (with errors in the original):

Are you tired of the situation on Center Street?
Trash, loitering, overcrowded housing, public drunkenness and urination.
Please pull together with your neighbors and join us at the town meeting.
Help save your neighborhood before it gets worse!

But much of the second page of the flyer was lifted directly from the FAIR website and used language that had previously not been a major part of the debate.

Love Jupiter? THEN LET'S SAVE IT.
*Are you tired of the blighted neighborhoods increasing on the southside of Center Street?
*Do you wonder what is happening to your neighborhood? Have you found yourself counting the number of illegals that line Center Street every morning?
*Are you worried that your property value may decline or you won't be able to sell at all?
GET THE FACTS
1. Illegal immigrants are a NATIONAL epidemic.
2. They are driven to stay illegal to make more money with nontaxed dollars.
3. Contractors may or may not realize they are contributing to the problem [by] hiring them.

4. Only 2% of the hiring takes place by a resident who needs occasional yard work.

5. Landlords are capitalizing with cash, renting to them sometimes 10 or 20 to a household.

6. Statistically, a CENTRAL HIRING LOCATION WILL NOT WORK. Illegals spread out to <u>increase their chances</u> of being chosen for work. Crowding 300 at a time into a building, will hinder their chances for employment. Only 1 in 10 will work on any given day.

7. Lastly: statistically, when the population rises into the thousands: <u>drugs, gangs, and inevitably crime escalates</u>.

It would be a crime for us, as taxpayers to support a Center that we think will eliminate a problem that shouldn't exist in the first place, <u>and it won't solve the housing issue</u>.

It is a slap in the face to all immigrants, who came to America, worked hard to earn their citizenship, who pay taxes and contribute as we all do for the benefit of our communities.

Don't turn a blind eye simply because you live in a section of Jupiter that doesn't have to see it everyday. <u>It will still effect you, because your tax dollars are paying for them.</u>

<u>JOIN US IN Support at the Council Meeting on Tuesday, December 7, Jupiter Town Hall, 7 p.m.</u>

On December 1, the day following the speech of the FAIR representative to Center Street residents, the Town Council received several e-mails filled with FAIR talking points about immigration. One individual who contacted the mayor wrote, "I have watched the numbers of illegals grow, while their respect for Town of Jupiter residents has diminished. Last year, there appeared to be the significant increase in illegal women as well, and now, I am seeing their children increasing in numbers."

Preoccupation with the fertility of immigrants is standard fare for FAIR. On its website FAIR argues that "immigration-driven population growth is straining our environment and quality of life" and stresses children born of immigrant parents as one of the main culprits contributing to this "problem." The e-mail to the council quoted above further elaborates on the issue of immigration.

I was asked by a friend to accompany him across the street, to assist him in hiring several men for full-time positions. We were swarmed by dozens of men, until I announced that the full time job was theirs for the taking, as long as they could produce a green card and a Social Security card. Without exception, every one of them turned and went back to their respective "pickup spots," apparently waiting for anyone who failed to realize that hiring illegal aliens for cash is a serious crime in itself. We talked to no less than 75 to 100 men, and they all passed on the full time job offer.

This tactic is also taken directly from FAIR. On its website, it makes available a guide for people seeking to oppose hiring halls in their communities. The guide suggests the following: "Since facts about legal residence cannot be established based on appearance alone, immigration reform activists can pose as prospective employers and hire workers from these hiring halls. Once the hiring has taken place, the employer must verify the legal status of the employee. If, as is often the case, the employees cannot produce valid documentation that is evidence that the hiring hall and its operators are acting in reckless disregard of the law." Another Jupiter resident contacted the Town Council on December 2, saying, "My husband has gone to the Jupiter office of Corn Maya to try to employ a 'legal' worker, but they were unable to recommend even one man!" Evidently, within days of the FAIR representative speaking in Jupiter, the strategies promoted by this organization were being implemented locally.

Members of JNAIL attended the December 7 Town Council meeting in large numbers. Also in attendance at this meeting was David Caulkett, representing Floridians for Immigration Enforcement (FLIMEN), an anti-immigrant group based in Pompano Beach (approximately fifty-five miles south of Jupiter). On the FAIR website, FLIMEN is listed as an affiliate organization that local groups can reach out to for help in addressing immigration-related concerns in their areas. David Caulkett, the FLIMEN representative who attended the Town Council meeting in Jupiter, also serves as Florida state adviser for FAIR.[9]

The Jupiter residents who opposed the idea of a labor center and sympathized with JNAIL, FLIMEN, and FAIR also contacted their U.S. congressman, Mark Foley. At the time, Foley was also deputy majority whip. Foley sent a letter to Mayor Golonka on December 22, expressing his "deep concern over the proposed development of a labor resource center on Center Street" and stating his belief that opening such a center in Jupiter would send a message "to both the rest of Florida and the nation that the Town of Jupiter sanctions illegal immigration." He made no reference to the original neighborhood issues that arose in Jupiter; rather, his focus was on larger federal immigration policy issues. He stated that "there are currently millions of illegal immigrants who live, work and have families in the United States. These aliens have not only broken the laws by residing in the United States, but they have put an enormous strain on both our economy and our healthcare system and pose a national security threat." The Foley letter was broadly covered in the South Florida media and put Jupiter's day labor issues in the center of a larger immigration debate.

The year 2004 came to an end in Jupiter with tensions running high. By the beginning of 2005 it had become clear that the Town Council had to act. Although they had approved the housing ordinance and started more aggressively enforcing code issues, the emergence of JNAIL and the appearance of FAIR in the local scene signaled a disturbing trend for Town Council members. It was clear that doing nothing was no longer going to suffice in Jupiter. But just as JNAIL had formed to oppose a resource center in an organized manner in 2004, the group of Jupiter residents who supported the idea also began to come together in 2005 to make their voices heard. The immigrants themselves also began to step forward and articulate their needs and role in the process. The story of their arrival in Jupiter, their own struggle to become part of the community, and their mobilization in favor of the Center is equally compelling.

2

The Immigrant Community in Jupiter

From Migrants to Mobilized

Jupiter's immigrant community was well aware of the growing tensions surrounding the Center Street day labor market and charter neighborhoods. As residents of the same neighborhoods, immigrants were also seeking solutions and points of contact to bring their perspectives to the table. In time, some of them began to emerge as community leaders, well positioned to represent the immigrant community because they could communicate with their fellow migrants, as well as their native-born neighbors and town authorities. Most had survived a brutal civil war in Guatemala and had undertaken tremendous risks in coming to the United States. Now they sought to maintain a foothold in both countries. To continue the cultural customs and traditions that bound their community together, in the early 2000s migrants in Jupiter began to organize, arranging soccer matches, requesting Spanish-language church services, and planning the celebration of the most important annual festival in their community of origin. In the process, migrant organizers began to build bridges to Jupiter's larger community that would be critical to the creation and success of the El Sol center.

MIGRATION THROUGH THE EYES OF A REFUGEE

No single individual better represents that process than Jerónimo Camposeco, one of the original migrants who came to Jupiter from Guatemala. Born in the late 1930s in the Guatemalan highland community of Jacaltenango, Camposeco understands the connections between Jupiter and Jacaltenango from a unique and multifaceted perspective. As a boy growing up in this agricultural community located on the slopes of the Cuchumatan Mountains in the department of Huehuetenango, he could never have imagined himself living in a place like Jupiter, Florida. As one of the oldest and longest established of the Jacaltecos living in Jupiter, his story brings to light many of the complex forces that link the two communities and underlie the larger process of migration from Central America to the United States.

As Camposeco explains, the need to move in order to survive has a long tradition within his home community.

> Most of the Maya people who live in the highlands are organized in municipalities on very small plots of land. Due to the altitude, the cold weather, land erosion, and the difficult nature of the terrain, a lot of the land the Maya work produces just one harvest per year. In order to supplement these yearly harvests, the Maya have often migrated. Traditionally the Maya went from the highland to the coast, where the coffee, cotton, and sugarcane plantations are located, to work as seasonal agricultural workers. These seasonal migrations were not easy; there were little to no means of transportation between the highland and the lowland, and people often had to make the long journey on crowded buses or trucks or by foot.[1]

Jacaltenango, Guatemala (Courtesy of Marcos Cota Diaz)

Jerónimo Camposeco at the Fiesta Maya, 2005 (Courtesy of Timothy J. Steigenga)

The lowland farms of Guatemala hold much in common with the climate, work, and geography of South Florida, but it was not these similarities that drew the first Mayans to the area. Instead, as Camposeco points out, it was a combination of forces, including Guatemala's genocidal civil war, multiple natural disasters, a lack of local alternatives, and networks of knowledge and support that began with the early migrants. Understanding these forces sheds light on how the department of Huehuetenango has become one of Guatemala's most prolific migrant-sending areas and how it is that almost one million Guatemalans (nearly a tenth of the entire population of Guatemala) now reside in the United States.

After leaving his village to attend a seminary as a young man, Camposeco returned to Huehuetenango in 1960 to serve as a schoolteacher at the Acatec Parroquial School in San Miguel Acatán. It was here that he met some of the very first Mayan migrants who would establish the networks linking the area to locations in the United States. Prior to 1976, migration from Guatemala was generally limited and primarily made up of urban workers and *ladinos*.[2] This first small wave of Guatemalan migration to the United States was prompted by the collapse of the Central American Common Market in the 1960s. In the face of economic hardship, some middle- and upper-class Guatemalans arrived in the United States seeking opportunities for personal and familial development.

In 1976 a 7.5-magnitude earthquake struck Guatemala's major fault line, killing about twenty-five thousand residents of the country's predominantly Mayan western highlands. Many survivors lost their jobs and homes. While some went to neighboring villages or Guatemala City, others sought new opportunities in the United States, thus beginning what was to become a large-scale and increasingly Mayan international emigration. By the end of the decade, according to Camposeco, "There were about thirty Akatekos in Los Angeles. This began a network of Mayan migration from Huehuetenango to the West Coast of the United States."

Although the earthquake served as a catalyst to migration, Guatemala had begun to experience severe social and economic unrest decades earlier. Following the U.S.-sponsored 1954 coup overthrowing the country's democratically elected government, Guatemala suffered a series of military dictatorships and a civil war that lasted from 1960 to 1996. The government's utter ineptitude in dealing with the further chaos caused by the earthquake prompted Guatemalans to begin migrating to the United States in large numbers. Furthermore, the violence worsened with the presidency of Efraín Rios Montt in 1982. Although he was only in power for little over a year, under his presidency the government pursued a vicious counterinsurgency campaign targeting suspected guerrillas. As Victor Montejo recounts in his 1999 memoir *Voices from Exile*, under the Rios Montt regime "all Mayas were suspect."[3]

It was in this context that Camposeco was forced to flee Guatemala. After completing his degree in education, he took a position working for the National Indigenous Institute in Guatemala City, a job that took him around the country and put him in contact with other Native American groups in North America and Mexico. In the eyes of the Guatemalan government at the time, however, Camposeco's work was subversive. After receiving notice that he was being sought by the military, he and his family fled the country and were taken in by a Native American group working in Pennsylvania.

Camposeco's departure from Guatemala corresponded roughly with the second wave of Guatemalan immigrants in Florida, which occurred in the years immediately following the earthquake, when the violence of the civil war reached its apex. Thousands of Mayan people fled, arriving first in Mexico, then crossing the border into Texas and California, and later moving on to Florida. Camposeco explains how networks and connections facilitated this process.

Many Mayas saw their livelihood severely threatened, and many were victims of violence at the hands of the Guatemalan army. Many people left their hometowns to escape the violence, and a number of them went to the United States, following the already established network of migrants. Some of the Guatemalan Maya refugees also went to refugee camps supervised by the UN and the Mexican government; others dispersed to different places. Some of these migrants in Mexico eventually fled to the United States. Others traveled across Mexico to the northern part of the country and found farmwork in Hermosillo, Caborca, and Culiacán picking vegetables with other native Mexican farmworkers. It happened that many of the Mexican farmworkers who worked with the Maya were frequent travelers to farms in the state of Florida in the United States during the harvest season. They invited the Guatemalans to cross the Arizona desert and the U.S.-Mexico border to go work with them in Indiantown, Immokalee, Fort Myers, and Lake Worth in Florida. By the early 1980s, the networks of Mayan migrants became major pathways for new refugees from the violence in Guatemala and the despair of the camps in Mexico. The work that I was doing in Guatemala with Native American tribes put me in danger as well because the Guatemalan government was suspicious of all organized groups during the height of the civil war.

In the 1980s many of these early refugees began applying to bring their family members to join them. Although they were concentrated primarily in Indiantown, just half an hour from Jupiter, these new Mayan immigrants also began to move to other South Florida communities, including Immokalee, Lake Worth, Stuart, Fort Myers, Bonita Springs, Naples, Port St. Lucie, Boynton Beach, Lake Worth, West Palm Beach, and Jupiter. It was during this time period that Camposeco first came to Florida. In 1983 the Indian Law Resource Center, based in Washington, D.C., was seeking an interpreter who could speak both English and Q'anjob'al, a Mayan language spoken primarily in Guatemala and Mexico. A group of Maya Q'anjob'al migrants in Indiantown were facing deportation and needed help in explaining their situation. With sponsorship from the Indian Law Resource Center, the Mohawk Nation, and a Mohawk newspaper called *Akwesasne Notes*, Camposeco served as interpreter for the detainees in their petition hearing for political asylum. In Indiantown itself, he notes, several local groups, including the Quakers, the Catholic Church, and Florida Rural Legal Services, began working to educate immigrant farmworkers about their rights and to defend them from abuses by employers and authorities.

Events in Indiantown in the 1980s would foreshadow much of what was to come almost twenty years later in Jupiter. As a small minority in a foreign and hostile place, the Mayan immigrants in Indiantown turned to their traditions for mutual recognition and support. Camposeco describes the process.

> The Maya people in Indiantown also wanted to socialize with each other. They were very nostalgic and missed their hometowns in Guatemala very much. Looking to help people cope with their grief, the leadership decided that re-creating some of the traditional celebrations would help people. One of the most important traditions is the celebration for the patron saint of the pueblos. In this case, because most of the people in Indiantown were Migueleños, they decided to celebrate the Fiesta of San Miguel Acatán, which takes place at the end of each September. The first fiesta was celebrated in September 1983. Some of the refugees were musicians, so we were able to perform live music at the fiesta. During the fiesta, the people were able to celebrate their cultural traditions, and women were able to wear their traditional clothes. We re-created in Indiantown during one weekend several aspects of a festival that lasts eight days in Guatemala. On Saturday evening after the mass, there were performances with poems, songs, the crowning of the queen, games, and social dances. On Sunday there were also soccer games with Guatemalan teams and Mexican farmworkers. The queen was present, the marimba group played traditional songs, and people enjoyed traditional food. This celebration has now taken place for many years in Indiantown.

Work on the fiesta helped to facilitate work on social programs in Indiantown. As he would later in Jupiter, Camposeco played a key role in this process, joining with local religious, civic, and academic leaders to found Corn Maya Inc.—the same organization that would later move to Jupiter. In Indiantown, Corn Maya worked with migrants, processing immigration claims, providing other social services, and facilitating the practice of Mayan cultural traditions.

In 1996 the civil war in Guatemala officially ended with the signing of the peace agreements. However, the problem of violence persisted, and the social unrest and economic chaos caused by the war continued to make life in Guatemala extremely difficult, especially for rural Mayans. It is not surprising, then, that the wave of Guatemalan immigrants who came to Florida in the 1990s was made up of primarily Mayan rural workers. Most were men (though recently more women have been coming) between the ages of fifteen and thirty-five, with either primary- or middle-school levels of education. Only a few had any hope of becoming legal residents, as most of them came after the war ended and thus did not qualify for refugee or asylee status.

Their different status forced changes on the organizations serving the immigrant community, including Corn Maya. Corn Maya had formed in Indiantown in response to the immigration policies of the early 1990s. In 1990 the INS had settled an important lawsuit brought by the American Baptist Churches on behalf of some Central American migrants whose asylum claims were being dismissed because the United States supported the governments that perpetrated the abuses the refugees were fleeing. As a result of the settlement, the INS agreed to revisit claims that previously had been denied. That same year, as part of the Immigration Act of 1990, Congress established a procedure by means of which the attorney general may provide "temporary protective status" (TPS) to immigrants who cannot return to their home countries safely due to armed conflict or other extraordinary circumstances. Corn Maya helped people with the application process for these programs. When the organization could no longer fulfill its original mission, Camposeco explains, it narrowed its focus to social services, cultural events, and sports tournaments. Meanwhile, as Indiantown's migrant population grew, some migrants began to seek work in nearby Jupiter. There they found jobs in construction, landscaping, golf course maintenance services, restaurants, and day labor.

Mayans on the Move: Migration as a Multicausal Process

As Camposeco's story makes clear, the forces propelling migration from Guatemala are multiple and complex. First, the earthquake and civil war drove hundreds of thousands of refugees out of their homes in the 1980s and 1990s. More recently immigrants to Jupiter have come fleeing not violence but poverty. Poverty in Guatemala is devastating. In 2009 the per capita gross domestic product (GDP) in Guatemala was $5,200 compared to $46,400 in the United States. The "wage gap" is even wider in some of the rural communities of Huehuetenango, where the minimum wage for agricultural workers is as low as $8 per day. The gap in earning potential is a powerful driving force of immigration.[4] Rebeca, a young Jacalteca woman we spoke to in Jupiter, explained the logic: "It was very difficult over there. It's not that making money is easy here, but when you take into account exchange rates and all . . . one thousand dollars goes very far over there . . . and you don't make that kind of money working there."

Rebeca's hometown of Jacaltenango is a predominantly agricultural town of approximately thirty-four thousand residents. The primary crops produced in

Jacaltenango are corn, beans, coffee, and avocados. The large majority of the population is Mayan, and many speak Jacaltec, as well as Spanish. Traditionally, houses in Jacaltenango were adobe homes with dirt floors and minimal internal divisions. Many Jacaltecos still live below the poverty line, with an income of less than a dollar a day. While the main economic activity is agriculture, Jacaltecos also work in a variety of trades, from carpentry to masonry. Earning a living from agriculture alone has become increasingly difficult in that area of Guatemala, in part because land has become more expensive as the families of migrants have invested in land with their remittance dollars. In general, opportunities for economic advancement in Jacaltenango are limited and earnings are low. A construction worker in Jacaltenango earns significantly less than one doing the same work in Jupiter.

While wage differentials are an important factor propelling migration, there are other complex economic, social, personal, and political forces at play that significantly impact a migrant's decision to leave. As Camposeco's account illustrates, social networks are among the most important factors affecting decisions to migrate. Guatemalans have been migrating to the United States for decades, and in the process they have built networks that facilitate further migration. Migration is risky and costly, but social networks help decrease this cost.[5] Often these migrant networks are family connections. Cousins, uncles, sisters, brothers, and fathers facilitate the journey for their families. Alba, a Jacalteca in Jupiter, explained how her family networks helped her during her crossing and on arrival: "The first time I tried to cross, a man robbed me of my money and I never saw him again. My sister then spoke to someone she knew, and they went to get me in Chiapas—then we crossed through the desert in Arizona. . . . I work because of my sister. She already knew a lot of people, and she introduced me to the lady for whom I work now."

Ulises, a young man whose life has been dramatically changed by El Sol and whose story we detail in chapter 5, recalls vividly the hardships he faced and the critical role that family networks play in facilitating migration.

I have been here three years, three months, and five days, to be exact. I am still counting. I got here on December 28 of 2007. I left Guatemala on December 14 from San Juan la Laguna, Solola. I left my house at around 3:00 or 4:00 p.m. I have two sisters that I haven't seen since that day. My dad brought me to a place called Cuatro Caminos in Guatemala so I could see my mom and my aunt. My cousin came with me, my cousin José. We came together. It was a similar story with him, it was his mom who was supposed to come, but they had a two-year-old girl, so his mom could not come. José was fourteen years old; he is seventeen now. We met up in that place. We were all sad. We were chatting a little bit. We went to a store to buy gloves, hats, and things like that to prepare for the trip. It was winter. We prepared as best as we could. My dad stayed there. My aunt and my mom came with us to the coyote's house. We got to the coyote's house, they fed us dinner, and we went to bed. The next day we woke up at 5:00 a.m. They put us in a bus and we went to the central park of Totonicapán. There we met two other coyotes. They were all organized: the boss, the subcontractors, everything like that. We met with these two other coyotes, we talked for a couple more minutes with my mom and my aunt, we said bye, they put us on the bus, and we turned around to see our moms one last time. They stayed there. I cried. I don't remember if José cried. We were very sad. We didn't know what the future held. We knew it was risky. We didn't know if we would make it, if they would deport us, or if we would die in the desert, in Mexico. It was something like a double-edged sword. So . . . we went to Huehuetenango. On the way there I was thinking so many things. I was already doubting it—should I go back home? I had never seen the places we were going [to]. I had never seen Huehuetenango. I had been to Quetzaltenango and to Guatemala City, but I had never seen the northwest region of Guatemala. It was like an excursion that at the same time for me was sad. I was afraid. At the beginning I was somewhat excited, but more scared.

In Mexico, frequently the most dangerous part of the journey, the coyotes prepared Ulises and José to cross the border posing as Mexicans.

We got there, and we went to another house. I imagine it was another coyote's house. Other people came in, like two more people. They gave us instructions about crossing the border, and they gave us instructions about Mexican ways of doing things. We learned common Mexican phrases, how Mexicans walk. Supposedly Mexicans dance a little when they walk. It was funny at that time. We all laughed a little when the coyote showed us how to walk like a Mexican and put on a Mexican accent. I was so nervous, and there were too many things to remember. They gave us false Mexican identification. My name was Ulises.[6] José also had a different name. We had to learn a date of birth, a set of parents' names, a place of birth, and all that. We had to memorize those things in case Mexican immigration stopped us and asked. I was so nervous that I never learned those things. I never memorized it.

Ulises and José's journey across Mexico was harrowing. They were separated almost immediately into different vehicles on the way to their first safe house in Mexico. Once they were reunited, they trudged for hours through the night to board the next vehicle. Stopped multiple times by Mexican immigration officials along the way, they miraculously escaped questioning each time. After nearly a week on the road, they arrived in San Luis Potosí, Mexico, nearly starved. Their coyote offered them food, but it was rancid, as it had made the same weeklong trip they had. They boarded yet another bus for Monterrey and transferred to a safe house in Reynosa—where for the first time since their journey started they were offered edible food and drink. From the safe house they joined yet another coyote and made a night crossing of the Rio Grande. Ulises describes the next stage of their journey after they swam across the river.

> The worst thing was crossing the desert walking. . . . They dropped us off in the desert; we jumped a fence and started walking. We were walking on sand. I was tired after fifteen minutes. I was so thirsty. They told us we were going to walk the rest of the day and all night. I was dead! Walking on sand is so exhausting. We saw human remains in the desert. I started wondering if I was going to end up like that or if I would make it across . . . but I made it, thank God. We stopped to eat; it wasn't a great dinner, but it was something. We didn't want to continue. When we stopped to rest for a bit, we just didn't want to continue. It was terribly painful. At night we couldn't see well. We couldn't have a flashlight. There were thorns everywhere. I was with my cousin, and I was the older one so I was in charge of him. It was hard, but I did it. He was behind me. I would touch around and warn him about the thorns and stuff like that. I would tell him to move to the side. We were walking in a row, and there were branches. The people who were in front of me would run into the branches and the branches would snap back and hit me! It hurt a lot, so I would tell José to duck and be careful. In the desert José couldn't walk anymore; he started vomiting. I told the coyote to wait, to stop and wait because José was vomiting. The coyote said no and kept walking. I stayed with José. I told the coyote that he had to wait because if he didn't I was going to start screaming and the police would help us with José but take him to jail for human trafficking. The coyote waited then; he even helped us. The coyote

helped us to remove the thorns from José. I took advantage of the break, and I lowered my pants, too, and began removing the thorns. I preferred the big thorns because you could touch them and remove them. The tiny thorns were much harder. They are so small, and I have no idea how they went through my jeans. I could not get them out of my jeans. When I was walking it hurt so much when the pants rubbed against my skin. It hurt a lot. The desert lasted all night.

After their walk through the desert, Ulises and José were taken to another safe house, in Texas. Although they had already paid for their trip to Jupiter, they were now informed that they would have to come up with more money for the last leg. As Ulises explains:

In the United States, we arrived to McAllen, Texas. I knew I was going to Jupiter because my uncle lived here. My uncle and one cousin, they were the reason we were headed to Jupiter. Anyway, we made it to Texas with the same coyote that we left San Juan with. So they were supposed to bring us to Jupiter, but in Texas they told us that they needed more money. We had already paid around six thousand dollars each. That's a lot of money. It's something that when you think about it, it might seem illogical to spend that much money. So, the coyotes said they needed more money. They wanted five hundred dollars more to get us to Jupiter. We called Guatemala; they didn't have the money. They called my uncle, and thank God he had some money saved. The agreement was that they would bring us here to Jupiter and then my uncle would give the coyote the money.

The experiences of Alba, Ulises, and José are common among the Maya in Jupiter. Few migrants would consider leaving their hometowns unless they knew someone or had some contacts to help them along the way and on arrival. Networks, especially family networks, are extremely important for understanding migration because many people migrate to reunite with family members who are already in the United States. Alba, for example, made the decision to migrate after her husband died. The idea of reuniting with her sister after such a loss was one of the driving factors behind her decision to leave. Arcadio, another Jacalteco in Jupiter, described the role family played in his decision to migrate: "My father went ahead and came [to the United States] in 2001, and I was left with my brothers—after one year, I came too."

Family is an important factor in migration not only because it can provide access to networks but also because the decision to migrate is often made not by the individual but by the family as a whole.[7] A family may decide that it is best to send someone to work in the United States in order to secure capital for investment, or as a type of insurance to diversify risk (if the price of coffee goes down or there is a bad crop, the migrant's income should still be available). Many migrants living in the United States use their earnings to cover basic life expenses and send all that is left to their families in Guatemala. These remittances are then invested in land, education, or a house. As Arcadio explained, "I don't have a house yet, but I know you have to work hard to get one. That's also why I came . . . to help my dad with my brothers and sisters, because he cannot support all of us on his own. I migrated to help them, to buy some land, and to work. . . . I want to accomplish many things. I want to buy a house, [and] land, and finance my siblings' education." Ulises migrated when he was seventeen, hardly old enough to make such a decision on his own. He explains the role of his family in the process: "We had planned it for about a year. My family's financial situation was not good. My dad had a job, but it wasn't much. He was supposed to be the one to come to this country, but because of his job, and the family and some other issues, we decided that instead of him I would come."

Migrant Economics: Markets, Investments, and Demand

For many migrants, like Arcadio, Alba, and Ulises, migration becomes the only method of securing capital to invest in income-generating enterprises, or invest in education to increase the chances of their family's upward social mobility. In order to succeed in the local market, individuals must have access to capital for investments, and often migration is the best way to acquire such capital.[8] In a strange twist, the process of economic development in Guatemala actually drives some of the migration by disrupting the ways in which people traditionally acquire local capital. For example, free trade agreements such as the Dominican Republic–Central America Free Trade Agreement (DR-CAFTA) have jeopardized the livelihood of some small farmers who cannot compete with larger agribusinesses. As families lose income from agriculture, they consider sending a migrant as a strategy to diversify their financial risk and compensate for the lost income.

Interviews with many Guatemalans in Jupiter have also revealed how important the demand side of the equation is in the process of migration. The United States has developed a segmented labor market, with high labor demand at the bottom of the market.[9] Low-skill jobs in maintenance, agriculture, construction, and landscaping make up this niche for immigrant workers. These jobs present little chance for upward social mobility and have very low prestige, so over the decades they have become increasingly undesirable for native-born workers. While jobs at the bottom of the segmented labor market carry a stigma for native-born workers, the opposite is true for migrant workers. These jobs carry a degree of prestige for migrants as they represent a path toward upward social mobility in their countries of origin. Not surprisingly, we found that Jupiter's migrants are well represented in these kinds of jobs. Arcadio told us about the types of jobs he has held during his time living in Jupiter: "The first and second month I was here, I started looking for work, and I found work at a landscaping company where I worked cutting grass. I was there for three months. From then, I went to work for a different company, planting trees. . . . I make seventy dollars a day." While his salary may seem low to an American worker, for Arcadio this money was sufficient for him to send nine hundred dollars a month to Guatemala and earn prestige as a good provider for his family.

Migrants like Arcadio, who send regular remittances to their hometowns, also become drivers of further migration. Simply put, families with migrants are able to build better houses and buy better things than families without migrants. These differences do not go unnoticed, and families without migrants are made more aware of their relative poverty every day. Traditionally, homes in most rural Guatemalan towns were small and made of adobe. Now some of these adobe homes stand immediately next to American-style houses that are several stories tall, with several bathrooms and individual rooms inside. Women in these communities used to cook their tortillas on a *comal*, a traditional griddle placed over an open flame, but now modern appliances and other consumer goods have made their way into small towns in Guatemala. All these new houses and modern appliances are only affordable to families that have a migrant sending remittances. Families without migrants do not have to go to the United States to see the American lifestyle firsthand. Young men in towns such as Jacaltenango are fully cognizant of all the potential improvements that migration would bring to the everyday lives of their families. As Julio, a young man from rural Guatemala now living in Jupiter, explained to us, "I came because I was not seeing any of the money from my work, and I could see the progress that the people who had migrated were making. They had fixed their houses, they had more money, and I could see it, and that's why I came." Migration, then, encourages more migration because it changes tastes, prices, and demands within sending communities, which, in turn, acts as a powerful motivator for young men and women to seek better things abroad.

Migration also acts as a conveyer belt that creates more migration in other ways. While people do purchase consumer goods with the remittance dollars they receive, a good portion of the money often goes into investments in such things as houses and land. The fact that some people have dollars with which to purchase houses and land drives prices well above what families without migrants can afford. As Julio explains, much of the land in his hometown belongs to migrants living in Jupiter: "They buy the land from here or they go there to choose the land. . . . They hire young kids to work there, and they get paid twenty quetzales per day [less than three American dollars]. . . . The migrant's wife administers the land." In this context, many of the migrants we spoke with felt that, although they would have much preferred to remain in their communities of origin, they had little choice but to move if they hoped to be able to support their families and dreams of a better life.

Increased enforcement along the U.S.-Mexico border has done little to deter potential migrants from Guatemala. In fact, most of the growth of the immigrant population in Jupiter has corresponded directly with the most intensive period of border enforcement in U.S. history, beginning under the Clinton administration and extending into the Obama administration. Despite the increased focus on the border and the detention and deportation of unauthorized immigrants, Jacaltecos have continued to arrive in Jupiter and other communities around the United States. In simple terms, as long as the demand for their labor and the networks that communicate that demand have remained intact, immigration has continued apace. As Douglas Massey and Jorge Durand have demonstrated in their studies of Mexican migration, the unintended effect of much U.S. immigration enforcement policy has been that immigrants who might otherwise circulate between their home communities and the United States are "locked in" because the cost of returning has become too high.[10] The Guatemalans we spoke to, like Julio, Ulises, Alba, and Arcadio, highlighted the fact that their debts and the difficulties of crossing were keeping them in Jupiter longer than initially expected. Almost unanimously the Jupiter migrants we interviewed initially came with plans to return to their country of origin after a few years of work. Economic factors and increased enforcement had caused them to stay beyond their initial plans for return.

Increased enforcement has also produced an atmosphere of fear within the migrant community. Throughout the course of our research, we heard of individuals who were left to deal with the aftermath of immigration raids, roadblocks, and traffic stops that led to detention and deportation. Migrant parents told us that they keep their children out of school for fear that they might be picked up on their way to or from classes. Many of the Guatemalans we met in Jupiter had been able to get driver's licenses when they arrived in the 1990s.

However, after 9/11 and the passage of the REAL ID act, few of them were able to renew those licenses, and subsequently a large number lost their insurance, their vehicles, and ultimately their jobs. Ironically, these were the individuals who were most settled, assimilated, and upwardly mobile among the new immigrant population in Jupiter.

COMMUNITIES LINKED ACROSS BORDERS

Although the path from Jacaltenango to Jupiter is long and dangerous for most migrants, the frequent travel, communication, and family connections across borders have joined these two communities in meaningful ways. Scholars of migration frequently refer to this phenomenon as transnationalism. In the broadest terms, *transnationalism* refers to activities, organizations, ideas, identities, and social and economic relations that frequently cross or even transcend national boundaries.[11] In the case of Jacaltecos in Jupiter, transnational connections are strong.

Migrants in Jupiter are in almost constant contact with Jacaltenango. Arcadio is typical in this respect. "I call my house every two weeks at least," he explains. "I buy a phone card, and I call. . . . I talk to my brother and my mother. . . . I'm interested in knowing how my brothers are doing, how my grandparents are doing, and what work my brother is doing." Arcadio's transnational identity goes beyond just getting news about his mother and brothers. When we spoke to him about his plans, they included a serious girlfriend back in Jacaltenango: "I would say [I'll get married] in two or three years. . . . I left her there with my mother to 'secure' her. We got together, and then I came here to build our house. I speak with her when I call my mother. She is twenty-two and does not work; she only helps my mom with my brothers. She speaks Jacaltec; she never went to school. I want to have two or three children with her."

Many young men like Arcadio live their everyday lives in between "here" and "there." Because of his own transnational identity and the everyday flow of information between the two communities, Arcadio lives his daily life in Jupiter, while simultaneously maintaining a solid bond with his family in Jacaltenango. In the face of a foreign and frequently hostile environment, Mayan immigrants in Jupiter turn to their primary sources of physical and emotional support: family, community, and church. In the process, they consciously and unconsciously adopt a survival strategy that entails the construction of deep and increasingly institutionalized transnational linkages.

In the case of Jupiter, these connections are best illustrated in the celebration of the Fiesta Maya, which was first celebrated publicly in Jupiter in 2002.

As in Indiantown, the roots of social mobilization among the migrant community can be traced back to the process of organizing for a cultural and religious event. The eventual evolution of El Sol can only be understood in the context of the early organization that went into planning and executing the fiesta.

FROM FIESTA TO MOBILIZATION

The first Fiesta Maya in Jupiter took place at Florida Atlantic University on January 27, 2002, and drew more than seven hundred community residents, primarily Guatemalan Mayans, for a day of cultural exchange, religious celebration, music, sports, and food. The fiesta was a "miniversion" of the Fiesta of Candelaria, the most important religious festival celebrated in Jacaltenango. In Jacal (as the Jacaltecos refer to it), the festival lasts about fifteen days in late January and

Soccer players at the Fiesta Maya, 2011 (Courtesy of Sandra Lazo de la Vega)

Dancers from the Dance of the Deer, Fiesta Maya, 2004 (Courtesy of Timothy J. Steigenga)

early February. This is a time filled with religious rituals. The town's queen is crowned, and a carving of the Virgin Mary is carried in a parade through the town on the last day of the festival (usually February 2). Different committees, such as sports and cultural, are formed for the festival. The town leaders assign somebody to be "captain" of the dance/theater group. This group practices arduously beforehand, so it is prepared for performances throughout the town. The dances the group performs include representations of the Spanish conquest, battles between the Christians and the Moors in Spain, and the hunt for deer. A few days before the festival's finale, the dancers accompany the people in the flower parade. During the flower procession women dressed in their finest clothing slowly walk through the town. The parade traverses the main streets until it reaches the church, where a priest blesses the flowers and the image of the Virgin.

The regional dance and child dancing, Fiesta Maya, 2011 (Courtesy of Sandra
Lazo de la Vega)

The festival concludes with a spectacular show of fireworks. One brave soul
straps a series of fireworks to his back and pretends to be a bull as the sparks
fly around him. The wealthiest families may hire specialists to construct wooden
"castles" covered with colorful fireworks that form the image of the Virgin or
other images related to the festival when lit. Each year a group of Guatemalans
from Jupiter collects money to construct a castle that says "Greetings from the
Jacaltecos in Jupiter, USA, to the Virgin of Candelaria in Jacaltenango." Soccer
and basketball matches are played, and dances are performed. On the final day
the council sponsors a dance in which men and women wear their best outfits
and dance to the sounds of the marimba, one of the most popular traditional
instruments of Guatemala.

For the Jacaltecos now living in Jupiter, memories of the Fiesta of Candelaria
reinforce the cultural ties to their hometown and also to each other. Jupiter's
one-day Fiesta Maya, inspired by the two-week festival in Jacaltenango, was
born of a desire to embrace this cultural heritage. Jerónimo Camposeco, who
had played such a pivotal role in organizing the Fiesta of San Miguel Acatán in
Indiantown, drew on that experience in organizing the first Fiesta Maya in

Jupiter. In both cases, he also drew on his firsthand knowledge of the fiestas in the two respective towns in Guatemala.

After the 2001 town meeting where the town manager convened stakeholders to discuss immigration and day labor, Camposeco continued to meet with university representatives to discuss opportunities for productive cultural and other exchanges among the immigrant community, the university, and the town. Initial conversations soon grew into a series of organizational meetings and plans for the first festival. After many meetings and hours of planning, the Asociación Maya Jacalteca de Jupiter was formed with a set of commissions, each responsible for different elements of the festival (flowers, music, food, etc.). These committees were similar to the organizational structure of the committees formed for the fiesta in Jacaltenango. The coalition of Guatemalans met weekly in the months leading up to the festival to prepare for the mass, procession, food, publicity, and other aspects of the celebration.

One of the Corn Maya board members who participated in the first fiesta explained the importance of both the fiesta and the shift from the Asociación Maya Jacalteca to the more general and formal status of Corn Maya Inc.

> When I first got here and we started trying to organize ourselves we each got specific roles. I was assigned to culture and sports. We started thinking about a fiesta. This helped us open up doors. If we had not identified ourselves as Corn Maya with a Fiesta Maya [as opposed to Candelaria], it would have been much harder for people to get to know us. The local authorities got to know us through the Fiesta Maya too. The university came to know us from that as well. I think the Fiesta Maya was a great event that changed us. We weren't people who were hiding anymore; we were not hiding underneath something anymore! When we did the Fiesta Maya, people knew us as Corn Maya. The name had a big impact too. If we had been the Asociación Maya Jacalteca it would have closed us up to others. It would have made it so that we were only geared toward the Jacalteco community. The name was wide enough and appeals to many people. The labor center was created after all this went on.

Patricio Silvestre is the president of Corn Maya Inc. and one of the initial leaders who worked with Corn Maya in Indiantown. As Silvestre explains it, the changing role of Corn Maya and the move from Indiantown to Jupiter followed the evolution of immigration policy in the 1990s.

Corn Maya in Indiantown formed because in '93–'94 there were several immigration policies, like ABC, TPS.[12] . . . Guatemalans could benefit from some of these projects. There was also a chance to get political asylum for some. Corn Maya helped people with the application process to get work permits. That was our main activity, and the organization was very active then. Corn Maya started becoming less and less active as the immigration programs that benefited Guatemalans stopped. Seeing that there was nothing to be done in Indiantown, the organization was transplanted to Jupiter. It started to operate in 2002 here really. Prior to being Corn Maya we used to be the Asociación Maya Jacalteca. We used to have this organization as Jacaltecos. We were not legally incorporated or anything, though, and we did not have 501(c)(3) status. When we would ask for permits from the city or something like that, a permit for the park or something, legally it was very hard because they wanted us to be a 501(c)(3). So then we started working with Corn Maya so that we could incorporate and be official. In 2000–2001 Corn Maya stopped functioning in Indiantown, and it started growing in Jupiter instead, as an organization that looked after the immigrant community.

FROM FIESTA PLANNING TO COMMUNITY MOBILIZATION

Following the first fiesta, the Corn Maya leadership began meeting on a monthly basis to discuss issues of concern to the immigrant community in Jupiter. Thus, in 2002, just as the town was becoming increasingly aware of the concerns bubbling up from the neighborhoods, the migrant community was also becoming more organized and able to articulate its needs and interests to town authorities. Thanks to research they conducted on other communities around the United States, the Corn Maya board members and town staff were becoming aware of how ugly the situation had become in some places with open-air labor markets, as well as the role that labor centers could play in mediating some of those tensions.

Patricio Silvestre describes Corn Maya's role in mediating relations between the town and the migrant community: "The city of Jupiter had a lot of problems with our community but did not have a person to talk to. They didn't have someone to call, someone to complain to. We started having good relationships with the town, and that's how we moved ahead." At the same time, the migrants had their own needs. "There were people who were waiting for work on Center Street. They were creating problems with the neighbors. We started concerning ourselves with those issues and started trying to solve them."

Members of Corn Maya had their own concerns about the open-air labor market. Day laborers had to stand outside under the hot Florida sun, without water or bathroom facilities. Unscrupulous employers could mistreat migrants with relative impunity and withhold wages for work that had already been performed. As Ulises explains: "They made me work, do things quickly. Sometimes they didn't pay you. Sometimes you had to work outside in the terrible heat, ninety degrees and more. . . . They didn't give us water sometimes; they didn't give you anything to eat. They discriminate against you. They see you here and they only look at you like you're an animal, less than an animal. People treat their animals really well here, but sadly not us sometimes. There are some people like that, not everyone obviously, but some people."

Furthermore, there was no standard way to determine who went out on jobs. Because employers were sometimes scarce, any car that drove up to the day laborers on Center Street could easily be overwhelmed by people looking for work, and from the workers' perspective the inability to determine whose turn it was to work also created tensions. As one of the Corn Maya board members pointed out, "I think that when there was only Center Street, before El Sol, the strongest person prevailed. The person who could climb into the car first went to work. Things have changed in that way. The opportunity is better distributed now. Things are more ordered now, and benefits have reached more people."

Another issue that affected immigrants severely was crime. While the Town Council heard claims from residents about immigrants committing crimes, more often than not Jupiter's immigrants were victims rather than perpetrators. A 2003 report by the Jupiter Police Department describes some of the problems that afflicted the immigrant community.

We have made great strides in opening up dialogue with the Guatemalan community, but there is still a feeling of mistrust on the part of the residents because they fear the police based upon personal experiences in their home country. We have held crime watch meetings for the community with poor attendance results. We have also printed pamphlets in Spanish alerting the workers to safeguard their money and not to carry large sums of money on their person in case of attempted thefts. While this has helped in some cases some of the workers have sometimes become the victims of robbery and theft, but we usually aren't notified about the occurrences because they are afraid to report it to the police because of illegal immigrant status or fear to contact police officials.

Some of the tensions arising in the neighborhoods came from cultural misunderstandings and a lack of communication. As Camposeco explains, "Newly arrived Mayan immigrants did not know very much about civic rules and ordinances, urban housing, language, and culture in Jupiter." Indeed, the Corn Maya leaders were distressed about many of the same problems cited by neighborhood residents. Silvestre elaborates.

> Our people went out waiting for work on Center Street. The town had complaints. We know—we are aware that we were not living in our country anymore, but we continued on with our same *costumbres* [customs]. There people wait for work, and sometimes when they had to go to the bathroom they would just go there, outside. That looks bad. That was a big complaint. In the end they wanted to move all these people, but to where? It was hard for us. When we went to meetings with you we could see that some Americans felt antipathy toward us. They didn't want us to be here. Unfortunately 9/11 happened. They started looking at us even worse; they started comparing us to those people. It was unjust.

Keenly aware of the issues causing tension in the neighborhoods, Corn Maya began working to address the concerns. Silvestre describes the organization's dual role in first fielding complaints and then conveying them to the migrant community.

> The complaints the neighbors had were about how we were violating the town rules and regulations. They wanted the neighborhoods to be quiet. When we had parties to celebrate birthdays and other things, they didn't like that, they had complaints. There were people who had families and children, and they were saying that their children could not go out and play because the neighbors were going to the bathroom outside. We started receiving all those complaints. They were saying that people were leaving trash all over the place; they were not recycling, etc. They also had complaints about people drinking in the street. There were many things that we had to inform our people about. They had to respect the traffic rules with their bikes, those who had cars needed to have licenses . . . all that information. The town had no way of relaying the information to the community. There was no organization to look after the immigrants.

Corn Maya came to be that organization. When town representatives brought in photographs of beer bottles lying around a neighborhood, Corn Maya informed the immigrant community about trash and recycling practices. Some-times, recalls Silvestre, immigrant residents would cover their windows with a sheet or a plastic bag, or would fix their cars and leave the parts lying around. "We started dealing with those issues house by house," he says. "We started explaining to people that they had to move things, clean up their houses."

At this point Corn Maya was still relying solely on volunteers, and in 2002 its board of directors began writing grant proposals for funding from the Commu-nity Foundation for Palm Beach and Martin Counties, Catholic Relief Services, and other organizations to provide office space for Corn Maya Inc.[13] While the board members were fully aware that the small grants they sought could not eliminate the simmering tensions in Jupiter, they hoped, at the very least, to provide a location with potable water and bathroom facilities where some day laborers could wait for work. Corn Maya also hoped to provide translation services, legal aid, and information on health care, and to offer a meeting space for those organizing cultural, educational, and sports activities. At the same time, it would continue in its role of facilitating communication among town officials, neighborhood residents, and members of the immigrant community.

In 2002 Corn Maya received its first grant from the Community Foundation for Palm Beach and Martin Counties and opened an office and pilot labor cen-ter in an industrial area near Center Street in May 2003. Almost immediately the Corn Maya office began to serve as a meeting place for members of the immigrant community. In its first year Corn Maya organized soccer tourna-ments, neighborhood cleanups, and community meetings from the office. The office gave a public face to an otherwise unrepresented group in Jupiter. Ulti-mately, Corn Maya helped to solidify and extend the bonds that had been formed during the planning stages of the first fiesta. Students from the Wilkes Honors College at FAU served as volunteers in the office, gaining valuable experience and a different perspective regarding in the difficulties facing the immigrant community. Students with Spanish knowledge aided in translation, paperwork, and English classes.

During that first year, members of Corn Maya also took a leading role in urging the Catholic diocese to address the fact that the church located closest to the immigrant community in Jupiter had no Spanish-language mass or des-ignated mission to the immigrant community. Silvestre explains that this was one of the early goals of Corn Maya: "There were a lot of us who were Catholics. We tried to make sure that those who were Catholic had access to churches; before mass was said only in English. We tried to talk to them, send letters to ask them to think of us, the poor and the migrants in Jupiter. That is how we

Workers and volunteers participating in a community cleanup, 2003 (Courtesy of
Timothy J. Steigenga)

started to gain some influence." A 2002 Corn Maya letter addressed to priest at
Saint Peter put the issue bluntly.

> As a community of faith with very traditional and strong Catholic values,
> we wanted to worship, practice, and share them in a congregation that can
> receive us as equals. Nevertheless, you did not include us in the convocation
> 15 years ago and you have excluded us to this very day. . . . You are one of
> us, our brother in Christ who doesn't know it, and we love our wayward
> brother. As you go to your powerful position in the prayer meetings you
> will ask that God be with you. Don't be mad at us for reminding you that
> there is no Holy Communion when people are excluded.

Corn Maya's letter came at an opportune moment. Bishop Sean O'Malley (now
Cardinal O'Malley) assigned Father Finney, Sister Marta, and the other Guadalupan sisters to Saint Peter in 2003, marking the expansion of the Catholic Diocese of Palm Beach's Hispanic ministry to Jupiter.

Shortly after Father Finney began celebrating mass in Spanish, the church
also initiated a social justice ministry. In early 2004, as the town was publicizing

the housing code changes, members of Saint Peter were beginning to meet to discuss how these changes would impact their new members from the immigrant community and what might be accomplished in terms of providing more affordable housing in Jupiter. As Father Finney explains, this was a transition for Saint Peter and represented a new way of thinking for the congregation.

> I remember a homily in that month before we started the Spanish mass. . . . I was the only priest here, so it was easy to speak at all the masses and get everybody all at once. There I remember first when we said that we needed to have a Spanish mass. I said how beautiful it is down here in Jupiter, so well maintained and everything. It is easy to drive by the guy who is trimming the median, the guy who is cutting the grass, the guy washing the dishes and washing the cars at the car wash, the guy building the house. It is easy to kind of walk by them or drive by them without seeing them. I said they were our parishioners . . . the majority of them were Catholic, they live here in Jupiter, and that we had the responsibility as Catholics to make sure that their needs are met, too, and to minister to them. I am not sure that people really saw it that way before. It wasn't necessarily that there was prejudice against them; I just think that people never realized that "Hey, these are Catholics and part of our family."

At the same time, Corn Maya was struggling to fulfill its initial goal of running a pilot labor center. It quickly became apparent that the small storefront office simply could not accommodate the nearly two hundred individuals who frequently lined Center Street looking for work each morning. Although the office was often full and more than a hundred people were placed into full- and part-time jobs in the first year, it was clear that the Corn Maya office was only making a small dent in the Center Street labor issue. Corn Maya could convince some day laborers to come to the office to wait for work, but as long as employers continued to go to Center Street, most workers would congregate there. The pilot program succeeded in demonstrating that workers would come to a structured location to wait for employment and that other nonprofit agencies would respond to a local agency able to articulate the needs of the immigrant community. Many of the programs and services offered at El Sol today are larger versions of what was offered at that first Corn Maya office in 2003 and 2004. English classes, legal assistance, visits from the Guatemalan consulate to assist with paperwork, maternal and child health counseling programs, neighborhood cleanups,

Board members of Corn Maya Inc. with a donated computer in the original office on Old Dixie Highway (Courtesy of Timothy J. Steigenga)

and public service opportunities were all initiated in the original Corn Maya office and expanded and formalized with the opening of El Sol.

As the office headed into its second year, Corn Maya focused its efforts on seeking public support and private funding for a larger public-private partnership with the town and other nonprofit organizations to open a larger neighborhood resource center. At the behest of the town manager's office, Corn Maya produced a formal five-year plan for a labor center in 2004 that outlined the history of its activities up to that point, a progress report, and a budget. The report read in part:

> The day labor project is a long-term project that can only succeed if the town, the police, and the immigrant community can maintain open lines of communication and a collaborative agenda. So far Corn Maya's relationship with town authorities has been very positive. We hope to carry that relationship into a future collaboration on a larger labor center site. If the town purchases or leases a property, the town will be investing

money in infrastructure to solve a town problem—not to serve a "special interest." Any services provided to the immigrant community will be fully financed and provided by nonprofit organizations such as Corn Maya. The investment in further property should be considered as an "extension" of the existing community center rather than a "separate but equal" facility. As such, the building should be open to all town groups who wish to use the space for programs and activities. The labor center has worked on a small scale at our office on Old Dixie Highway. A larger location combined with an enforceable Town ordinance on informal labor pick-ups at other locations will bring contractors and private individuals to the labor center. The common denominator in the success stories for other towns dealing with day labor issues is a cooperative public-private partnership between local governments, non-profit organizations, and funding agencies.

Back-to-back hurricanes in the fall of 2004 also highlighted the unique role that Corn Maya had come to play in the Jupiter community. In the days following direct hits on Jupiter from hurricanes Frances and Jeanne (just three weeks apart in September), the Corn Maya office was selected as a Federal Emergency Management Agency (FEMA) distribution center. Because Corn Maya had an existing office that was known throughout the community, it was a natural choice to serve as a distribution center. Corn Maya volunteers and FEMA staff provided food aid and tarps to Jupiter residents for weeks following the storms. Hundreds of residents of Jupiter's charter neighborhoods came to the Corn Maya office for emergency food and water. Corn Maya volunteers also rode on pickup trucks, delivering emergency supplies street by street through the charter neighborhoods, which were some of the hardest hit by the storms. In the weeks immediately following the storms, there was hardly a day laborer to be found along Center Street, as residents from Palm Beach and Martin Counties sought help with cleanup and repairs from the storms.

Forming a Broader Coalition

By 2004 lobbying for a larger, more permanent space—the future resource center—was taking place on multiple levels. On one level, an interdepartmental team of town staff and representatives of Corn Maya worked to share research and craft a multipronged approach to the most pressing neighborhood issues. Members of the group crafted a question-and-answer sheet about the operations of the center and briefed individual Town Council members. On another level, Corn Maya continued to seek grant funding and collaborative relationships from multiple organizations for a larger center and expanded programs and interns at the existing storefront center.

Since the Town Council was not yet ready to act, Corn Maya representatives accepted all invitations to speak to groups about the issue and to listen to groups that had neighborhood concerns. With tensions escalating, center supporters wanted to keep avenues of communication open with residents of the charter neighborhoods and other Jupiter residents. Multiple talks and informational sessions were held at Rotary Clubs, the Kiwanis Club, gated communities, and local churches and educational institutions in Jupiter and surrounding areas to inform Jupiter residents about the specifics related to a potential resource center.

It was at this point that a coalition of groups and individuals interested in supporting a resource center also began meeting in the offices of the Saint Peter Catholic Church. This group included parishioners who were part of the social justice ministry, members of Corn Maya, representatives of Catholic Charities, some neighborhood residents, Father Don Finney, Sister Marta Tobón, and representatives Rosa María Montenegro and Reverend Donald Duncombe from the Immigration Issues Committee of People Engaged in Active Community Efforts (PEACE). With prompting from PEACE, the coalition began to consider taking a more confrontational approach to the Town Council on the issue of a resource center. As Silvestre explains, this did not sit well with the board of Corn Maya.

Corn Maya's success has a lot to do with how open we are to working with other organizations. We want to work with everyone, and we will entertain any project as long as it fits within our mission. Maybe back then, in 2004 or so, we were desperate. Somebody mentioned to us that there was an organization in the Palm Beach diocese. The organization was called PEACE. This organization was powerful, but in their own way. They were people who wanted to organize a kind of uprising of the people against the town. There were several meetings with Corn Maya, Saint Peter, them, us . . . Sister Marta. . . . What happened was that this organization was good because they have political weight. They came and wanted us to drag some city employees in front of our people so that we could "cast stones" at them and yell at them. They wanted us to be more aggressive. They wanted a confrontation. We tried to work with them so that things didn't go that way. That was not the way Corn Maya did things. We were looking for more diplomatic ways of achieving our goals. We were going to meetings where the council was making decisions. We did work with PEACE, but when negotiations started, that option [of protest] was removed from the table.

As 2004 wound to a close, there was a growing sense of urgency as tensions continued to rise in the neighborhoods and along Center Street. Increasingly the immigrants themselves were becoming the targets of harassment and verbal abuse in Jupiter. While participating in a community cleanup along Center Street, Corn Maya volunteers suffered jeers and expletives shouted from passing cars. Shortly afterward, a one-ton dumpster full of garbage was overturned behind the Corn Maya offices. That same month someone placed an "illegal immigrant children at play" banner over a traffic sign near the Jupiter Elementary School in Pine Gardens South. As the incidents of intimidation intensified, the coalition asked those who had experienced them to write members of the Town Council and let them know what was going on. One such letter writer explained to the mayor:

I have been in South Florida for the past 22 years and have always felt it was my home. I thought I would live here for the rest of my life. I have resided in the town of Jupiter for the past four years. I have never been so disgusted, offended and have lost total faith in equal rights and progressive thinking. Our home is for sale and I can tell you: I cannot get out of Jupiter fast enough!! I am married to a wonderful Latin man who is a great asset to this community. We are both professional hard working people. He is management at [a local company], and I work [for the university]. We are prime examples of the immigration system success story. But sadly, Jupiter is a prime example of BACKWARD thinking, prejudice, subtle innuendos, etc.

After describing a series of incidents in which she and her husband experienced acts of intolerance in Jupiter, she went on to state:

The lack of tolerance and the lack of a clear understanding of what this country is founded on need to be addressed. The best way to educate people is to show them by action. If you take the initiative to help these Mayan people and in turn make Center Street a more desirable place for the "other half" to drive by without being offended, maybe their minds will open up and change. People automatically condemn things they do not understand, but I guarantee if they had to go through the unbalanced, almost impossible immigration process, they would have more compassion. These people are hardworking, honest, gentle people only looking for the same American dream we are all after. Please help them, not condemn them. We are all immigrants to America. Have you forgotten where your ancestors came from?

After discussion at the group meeting at Saint Peter, Father Finney also drafted a letter to the mayor urging action on the part of town authorities. Without such action, he warned, the possibility of further conflict was likely.

Mayor Golonka: I think the time to act is now. The situation in Jupiter is starting to turn ugly. I just received an email about the JNAIL group wanting to stand out on Center Street and videotape. Without some strong leadership from the council this situation is going to go from bad to worse and soon I fear will turn violent. I believe all the parties involved have the common denominator for wanting to make Jupiter the best place to live: A safe city, a beautiful city, a city that respects cultural diversity. Letting this issue simmer or ignoring it won't make it go away.

And he had come to a conclusion about the Federation for American Immigration Reform: "After doing more research on FAIR, I see that they are against ALL immigration to the United States, legal or illegal. This organization seems to have a very negative agenda and I would hope that residents of Jupiter would not base their views on the job center based on xenophobia. I am always willing to be of assistance and want only what is truly best for all involved."

In late 2004 tensions in Jupiter were reaching an all-time high. Just as the immigrant community began to assume a higher profile through the public celebration of the fiesta and a more prominent role within the local Catholic church, it found itself the target of verbal and other attacks in town. After almost four years of inaction by the Town Council, 2005 would usher in a period of intensified debate and ultimately a favorable resolution through the creation of a neighborhood resource center.

3

Debating a Community Resource Center

Respected members of Council, I am a medical person. If I were to discover
that I had a tumor that had been growing over the last two or three years,
I would take IMMEDIATE action. I would get at least *three* professional
opinions and act as soon as humanly possible. My very life could hang in
the balance. So please understand that I am confused and befuddled on
the speed of Council's response to the tumor that has invaded the Charter
Neighborhoods. We have identified the cancer. It *will* kill quality in these
neighborhoods. And to take the analogy further, it *will* metastasize into
other neighborhoods, ultimately threatening the viability and quality of
a beautiful town that is Jupiter. To bring this home to the issue at hand:
There is a hurricane rushing towards us and all I see are good-hearted
people passing out umbrellas on Center Street.

—January 2005 letter to the Town Council from a
Pine Gardens South resident (emphasis in original)

By the end of 2004, the issue of day labor had moved to the center of local politics
in Jupiter, and the Town Council was seriously considering the option of a labor
center. A December 29 guest editorial in the *Jupiter Courier* listed the center
among the most important issues concerning the town in 2004. The author of the
editorial, Roger Buckwalter, took a stand in favor of the center, warning, "The
Town Council must not cave in to some residents' vociferous attempts at intimidation, which is a terrible basis for making policy. It will take real 'profiles in
courage' to approve the Labor Center. But the town should do it."[1] But as Buckwalter noted, vociferous opposition to the center was reaching an all-time high as
the town entered the new year. Center opponents sought new allies and new tactics to put pressure on the Town Council. While Buckwalter's guest editorial was
supportive of the center, the *Jupiter Courier*'s full-time editor, Louis Hillary Park,
was a staunch opponent, and he penned a number of editorials opposing it.

Jupiter Neighbors against Illegal Labor (JNAIL), which had formed in 2004,
continued to hold meetings and write letters to the council. As detailed in

chapter 2, national (FAIR) and state (FLIMEN) restrictionist organizations also became involved in Jupiter, tapping into the frustration over the original neighborhood and day labor problems and framing the issue in terms of a larger anti-immigrant agenda. Representatives of FAIR made public threats to sue the town if it pursued the opening of a center, drawing significant coverage from local and national media. Congressman Mark Foley's letter in late 2004 urging the town not to open a center further polarized the issue. Letters and e-mails like the one that opens this chapter were arriving on council members' desks with greater frequency.

In January 2005 JNAIL organized the first protest of the proposed center at Jupiter's annual Jupiter Jubilee event on town property. The Jupiter Jubilee was initiated as part of Jupiter's seventy-fifth anniversary celebration in 2000 and is designed as a family event, with music, games, civic education, and cultural components. Approximately fifty protesters attended the 2005 Jupiter Jubilee waving signs and shouting slogans. The *Palm Beach Post* quoted one of the protest organizers suggesting a link between immigrants and terrorists: "We have no clue who these people are. . . . This country is not indestructible. People need to realize that 9/11 really happened. My motivation is to protect what my ancestors built."[2] The same individual stood up at a Town Council meeting later that month to display a large printout of Mohamed Atta's Florida driver's license as the council discussed the possibility of a labor center.

A town resident who had witnessed how the rhetoric had shifted around the issue of day labor wrote a letter to Congressman Clay Shaw, detailing the growing tensions in Jupiter: "Please do not allow the anti-immigration, hate-speaking group that has appeared in the Town of Jupiter to dictate to us what Jupiter officials should do regarding a Resource Center. I have been discussing this issue long before this group appeared in town. Before this group showed up with this hateful rhetoric there were enough votes on the Town Council to establish the Resource Center. Now some of those Councilors and the Mayor are backing down on their commitments." The coalition of organizations that opposed the idea of a labor center was growing, attracting people from different towns who found in Jupiter's situation a potential platform from which they could voice their concerns about immigration.

But 2005 brought several positive developments in the founding of a center as well. A number of Jupiter residents were uncomfortable with the sort of rhetoric being espoused by Congressman Foley, FAIR representatives, and JNAIL in the local media. Mike Richmond, a local resident, wrote to the *Jupiter Courier*, "I would like to express my strong agreement with Roger Buckwalter's insightful comments urging approval for a resource center for day laborers. . . . My hope for the New Year is that the Town Council will take note of the strong support that exists in the community for the day labor center (Neighborhood Resource Center) and will continue to work with interested organizations such as Corn Maya Inc. and others to make it a reality."

Richmond was one of the first residents of Jupiter outside the immigrant community to lend his full support to the idea of a labor center. As a resident of a development along Center Street, he had long been aware of the day labor issue. As a journalist who had worked for more than twenty years in San Diego and a former Senate staffer, he was very familiar with the larger issues surrounding the immigration debate. He quickly responded when Congressman Foley's letter to the town was reprinted in the editorial pages of the *Jupiter Courier*. In a January 2005 letter to the editor, Richmond stated: "The Jupiter Town Council and the Corn Maya organization . . . have been working in good faith towards the establishment of a neighborhood resource center and [are] making progress. And while there is opposition there are many others who are supportive of their efforts. We can only hope that Rep. Foley, R-Jupiter, and others will also lend their support and ideas to achieve a positive resolution that will make Jupiter serve as a model for other communities with similar concerns."

Richmond was also an active member in the Jupiter Democratic Club, which would come to serve as a critical source of support for the concept of a center. A January 2005 meeting of the club turned out to be a contentious affair. Panelists invited to this meeting included some of the leaders of JNAIL, a representative of Corn Maya (Tim Steigenga), and Jim Kuretski, a member of the Town Council. Also present in the crowd were several Center Street residents who opposed the idea of a resource center and had routinely been appearing to voice their concerns at Town Council meetings. As Kuretski explains, the atmosphere and events at the meeting had a significant impact on his approach from that point forward.

> We talked, and you [Steigenga] invited me to meetings. You invited me maybe three or four times, and you probably thought that I was never going to show up. I came to the Jupiter Democrats meetings, and I will never forget it. It was surreal when I walked in the room and I saw what the setting was. I remember going up, sitting by you, and still sitting there I could see how they were almost going after you. I didn't exist out there. That's when for the first time I understood what you had been going through. It was at that moment, that event. It struck me. . . . I remember

the anger and feeling bad about it. I thought, "I'm an elected official. I took on this job as a leadership opportunity. If I don't step up and be a leader and accountable, then shame on me.

During the meeting, questions were raised and answered about how the proposed center would operate, who it would serve (Jupiter residents), and some of the common misconceptions that were circulating about immigrants in Jupiter (e.g., that they were driving up crime rates). Opponents of the center repeated a combination of legitimate neighborhood complaints mixed with misinformation that came directly from FAIR. Richmond recalls: "I think it was at that meeting with the Jupiter Democratic Club where you [Steigenga] and Jim Kuretski spoke about the problem here and the need to do something. The feds weren't going to do anything locally, and having a Town Council member there who seemed to be interested, all that really got my attention. After that meeting several of us kind of huddled together to see if there were any volunteers who would like to do more, and that's how I got involved."

From this point forward, Kuretski stepped up as a council member and advocate for the center. In fact his advocacy, in combination with that of some key participants in the Jupiter Democratic Club, became the backbone of a group that would later be called the Friends of the Jupiter Neighborhood Resource Center. "The Friends," as it came to be known, would come to play a crucial role in advocating for the center and providing the core volunteers involved in the day-to-day operations of the El Sol center.

FRIENDS AND FOES

Immediately following the Jupiter Democratic Club meeting, a number of members met and proposed that the club take a stand on the issue of a labor center. The club voted unanimously to ask the Town Council to form a citizens' advisory committee made up of local stakeholders to suggest solutions. It was at this point that another key actor joined the coalition in favor of the center. Jill Hanson, vice president of the Jupiter Democratic Club, became an active advocate on behalf of the center along with her fellow club member Mike Richmond. Richmond and Hanson would go on to become the president and vice president of El Sol's first board of directors and to serve as its first two presidents. But at the time of the meeting, both had only recently become aware of the issues simmering in Jupiter. As Hanson explains: "I didn't really know anything about the immigrant community in Jupiter, much less that there was a problem until you guys [Kuretski and Steigenga] came to our Democratic Club meeting in

January of 2005. I had read about it in the paper, I think in late 2004. There was an article in the *Courier* and one of the council people was quoted saying, 'Well, I don't know why we should do anything about this problem. Nobody is coming here supporting the idea of doing anything about it.'"

Hanson quickly took that message to heart. Shortly after the Jupiter Democratic Club vote, she was interviewed in the local paper about the club's stance and noted that she would be among those who spoke in favor of the Center at the Town Council's next meeting. Although her own background was not in immigration-related issues, she had a long history of working for social justice.

> I was twelve or thirteen years old, went to Catholic school, and really believed everything they told me. That really influenced my whole life. I became involved in the civil rights movement when I was sixteen or seventeen years old in my hometown of Cincinnati. I stayed involved in that movement. I marched with Martin Luther King in Selma. [My husband] Sol used to say that was one of the reasons he married me . . . because I marched with Martin Luther King. . . . When I was in college I stayed involved with different social justice movements. I was involved in the movement against the war in Vietnam. After I graduated from college I became involved with unions when I worked at the Jewish Theological Seminary. I was one of the founding members of the New York City chapter of the Coalition of Labor Unions. We started a union coalition of all the academic institutions. I went to law school to become a union lawyer, and I did that for thirty years.

Hanson's husband, Sol Silverman, also became an outspoken advocate for the center. A former union organizer and important local political figure in the Democratic Party, he soon began using his political connections on behalf of the center. As with Hanson, his interest in the project sprang in part from personal experience. As Hanson explains:

> Sol knew from his background that these people had to be organized somehow or they would be constantly available at the bottom. He also knew more than that, just as a matter of humanity. He grew up during the Depression. His mom and dad were immigrants from Romania. His dad died when he was eighteen months old. When his dad died, his mom was left with four kids under the age of six. They moved in with her brother and sister and their two kids, and they all lived in a one-bedroom apartment.

Sol Silverman and Jill Hanson (Courtesy of Jill Hanson)

That was familiar to him from the situation here as well. . . . He never got the chance to really meet some of these people here at El Sol, but I think that in his heart he knew that their experience was very similar to his.

Hanson goes on to explain Sol's introduction to union organizing.

The way he tells the story is that after his first day of work, his mother told him, "I'm going to take you down, and you are going to join the union." So he did. He took the workers out on strike on the first job that he had— they were making ten cents an hour for sixty hours a week with no overtime pay. He became an organizer for the union. He organized all over the Northeast and in the South. He was always very active. MLK [Martin Luther King Jr.] was assassinated in 1968, and that same year they put in their collective bargaining demands that MLK's birthday had to become a holiday, and it became a holiday for his union. They thought that instead of the workers taking pay for the day, they would put it in a scholarship fund: MLK scholarship fund. His whole life he fought for integration, years before it was a popular thing to do.

Silverman had been a resident of Century Village in West Palm Beach and represented residents there in a dispute with a local developer. This experience gave him tremendous local political clout in Palm Beach County politics. Century Village represented nearly fifteen thousand mostly Democratic voters—a critical bloc for county elections. With Hanson and Silverman on board, supporters of the resource center now had contacts with county-level politicians and representatives of the labor movement.

At the February 1 Town Council meeting, Silverman and Hanson spoke in favor of the center. For the first time, the council began to see a more diverse group of speakers on the issue and attendees in the audience. The event made a major impression on those in attendance. Hanson explained, "All these Hispanic people came to thank Sol after the meeting because he had spoken for them. It was compelling for me personally . . . [and] it was a compelling need of the community that needed to be met."

The grassroots coalition made up of representatives of PEACE, Saint Peter, Catholic Charities, and Corn Maya, who had been meeting on a regular basis, gained new members and new life following the Jupiter Democratic Club meeting. With the addition of Hanson, Silverman, and Richmond, plus the now active participation of Kuretski, the coalition began producing documents and lobbying more aggressively in favor of the center. The group began to distribute information packets to potential supporters, which included background information on Corn Maya, Catholic Charities, the Friends, and supporters of a resource center. In an effort to inform Jupiter residents about the potential role of the center, the group circulated a document that included a summary of the history and background of the issues, a list of participating agencies (Corn Maya Inc., Catholic Charities, Saint Peter Catholic Church, the Guatemalan consulate, the Wilkes Honors College of FAU, and others), and the following description of what a resource center could accomplish in Jupiter:

> *Eliminate the Center Street Labor Market*: The resource center will provide a clean, orderly, and controlled environment for day laborers to gather to find work. Workers will be allowed to exit with employers based on a membership system. Only workers who reside in Jupiter will be allowed to make use of the center. Membership cards will include work experience and skills. Employers may call to request workers or simply

pull up to the building to request workers. Workers will be placed
with employers according to a first-come-first-served list system. In
conjunction with enforcement on Center Street, the center will address
safety and traffic concerns, significantly reduce the congregation on
Center Street, address nuisance complaints and garbage overflow issues,
and control unethical behavior by employers.

*Educate All Participants about Their Rights and Responsibilities as
Residents of Jupiter*: The resource center will inform employees and
employers about their rights and responsibilities in terms of taxes
(through individual tax payer identification numbers), workers
compensation, tenant and landlord rights and responsibilities, town
codes (overcrowding, oversize vehicles, and other codes), and health
and human safety issues (crossing intersections, bike safety, proper
sanitation and garbage disposal).

Offer Citizenship Training and Immigration Paperwork Assistance: The
center will offer training on citizen rights and responsibilities and will
provide assistance for eligible individuals with immigration paperwork.

Offer Services and Training to Laborers: For individuals who do not find
work or who seek to improve their skills, the center will provide English
language classes, legal assistance, computer classes, certification courses,
financial literacy training, and other related services.

Provide Community Service: Workers who wish to volunteer for community service will be automatically added to the top of the list for the next
day's labor pool. Community service workers can perform clean-ups in
troubled areas and can do neighborhood education on community
standards.

Offer Social Services: There is an ongoing need for basic social services and
referrals among Jupiter's immigrant community. The resource center
will serve as a central location for service agencies who offer maternal
child health assistance, legal services, family counseling, substance
abuse counseling, and other services.

Serve as an Outreach Center for Charter Neighborhoods: As with other
town-owned facilities, the center will be open to all neighborhood
groups and Jupiter residents for outreach, meetings, public forums,
and recreational activities. The center will provide a location for all
residents of Jupiter's charter neighborhoods to feel welcome, providing
a critical bridge for building trust and cooperation in the charter
neighborhoods.

The document also noted that while opening and operating a resource center would address the most visible tensions related to the immigrant community in Jupiter, it would not solve all of the underlying neighborhood problems. The coalition called for a comprehensive approach to the neighborhood issues that would include the humanitarian enforcement of health and human safety codes, alternative housing for displaced individuals, public transportation to reduce crowding problems by providing access to housing in areas outside of the charter communities, community policing (including increasing the number of Spanish-speaking officers on patrol in the charter neighborhoods), and hiring a Spanish-speaking neighborhood coordinator so that representatives of the Spanish-speaking population could be included in neighborhood meetings.

On the political front, the March 2005 elections also brought new voices into the debate. Don Daniels, the most vocal center opponent on the council, was initially challenged by David Harris, a center supporter who had been involved dating back to the original 2001 meetings with the town. Harris withdrew from the race for personal reasons, leaving Daniels to run unopposed. When election results were tallied, Harris had garnered 49.3 percent of the vote despite the fact that he had pulled out of the race well before Election Day. In the same election, Robert Friedman defeated Kathleen Kozinski to take her seat on the council. Kozinski had also been an outspoken opponent of the center both on the council and in the run-up to the election. Friedman, on the other hand, took a more measured approach, and he ultimately chose to donate a portion of his remaining campaign funds to the organizations that would come to run the center after his election.

During and after the election, coalition members also began to gear up for a demonstration of support for the center at the April 5, 2005, Town Council meeting. Jim Kuretski's wife, Terry, is a graphic designer and developed a logo for the group. The group planned to wear blue shirts with the logo to show support when the council was set to vote on a location for the center at the April 5 meeting. Two days prior to the meeting, members of the coalition and other stakeholders scouted potential sites for the center around town. By this point the members of the coalition were in agreement that the best potential location was the Lifesong Church building located directly across from the police station on the corner of Indiantown Road, the main thoroughfare through Jupiter. Fortuitously, the building was immediately adjacent to the larger campus of town properties, and the town was already under contract to purchase the building for the long-term expansion of its own offices. In other words, the town would be utilizing property that would otherwise sit empty in the short term.

The tour of potential sites brought together a unique combination of center supporters and opponents, neighborhood residents, town representatives, and other interested parties. Among those present was John Levin, the director of Catholic Charities, who had been attending the meetings at Saint Peter and had committed the assistance of Catholic Charities in running the center. Also present were Father Finney and Sister Marta of Saint Peter, Mike Richmond of the Friends, a young neighborhood couple who opposed the opening of the center, and a number of town staff and council members. As the tour came to a close, it was clear that the church building was not only the best location for the center but also the most politically feasible. Despite this consensus, the Town Council had yet to vote, and it was unclear how the members of the council, other than Kuretski, would vote on the issue.

For the first time since the issue was raised in 2001, however, there was a large coalition of center supporters prepared to show their support at the council meeting. As the "blue shirts" filed into the Town Council chambers on April 5, 2005, the group remained apprehensive about the vote. If a clear majority on the council could not be forged, town staff would be forced to go back to the drawing board on neighborhood issues. As Town Manager Andy Lukasik explains, he conceived his role not as a political leader but as "paid staff." Until center advocates had somebody who was "very, very strong" to take on the issue, it would be difficult even to discuss it in a public forum: "It was politically very hard to do what I wanted to do because I didn't have the support. Fortunately, Jim Kuretski was very strong. He was the one who pushed it over the edge. If it weren't for him, it wouldn't have worked. He did a lot of the grassroots stuff. This effort at the grass roots is what ultimately pushed it."

The atmosphere in council chambers was tense. As they had been since late 2004, the JNAIL members gathered in their red shirts. Ever since the January meeting of the Jupiter Democratic Club, members of the coalition had been working to recruit supporters to come to the meeting. Sister Marta and Father Finney worked through the religious community, students from the Wilkes Honors College recruited their classmates and professors, and Corn Maya spread the word to the immigrant community that this would be a critical meeting for the future of the town. At first the number of blue shirts and red shirts in the audience was about even. And, as usual, the council had other items to discuss before moving to the resource center. But as the evening progressed, the number of blue shirts continued to swell. When Andy Lukasik began his presentation to the council, approximately 50 more supporters, mostly members of immigrant families from Saint Peter and Corn Maya, quietly filed into the back of the room. At this point there were nearly 150 individuals there to show their support for the center.

As Andy Lukasik later explained, that moment was a major turning point in the struggle to found the center: "People in red shirts were saying that illegal immigration was ruining our community and that we weren't going to be Jupiter any longer. People in blue shirts started showing up saying that we needed a humanistic approach on this. . . . You started seeing the support. I think the grassroots thing was pivotal. The 150 people at the meeting were pivotal: it was the thing that turned the tide." Mayor Golonka agreed, citing the importance of visible support in the community for a positive solution to the ongoing issues. Participants in that dialogue, she recalls, "ranged from unhappy neighborhood people to people who thought we should be more involved from a social standpoint." What mattered was the groundswell of interest in finding a constructive approach. The community involvement, she explains, "allowed us to take a backseat and be a partner, but not in the lead."

Most of the individuals who attended the meeting did not ask to speak. The majority simply filed in quietly to the standing-room-only space at the rear of the chamber. As one of the Corn Maya board members explained: "People were talking about how it was supposed to be a protest. The guy who drove me to church told me it was a protest. Being present is different from protesting. I spoke to Sister Marta and told her that she could mobilize people but that she had to be careful in the way that certain activities were handled. We just wanted to gather support for our community; we didn't want to protest."

Following Lukasik's presentation, each council member made some comments. Mayor Golonka was still hoping for a site in the industrial area of town but indicated that the church building would be among her preferred sites. Councilmen Woodraksa, Kuretski, and Friedman concurred. Vice Mayor Don Daniels voiced his disagreement with the entire concept. As the conversation died down, Mayor Golonka noted that the consensus of the council was to place the church first on the list and to move forward the "neighborhood issues" raised by staff. Her pronouncement was met with grumbles and catcalls from the red-shirted opposition, and confused silence by the blue-shirted majority.

The public comment session immediately followed with a line of red-shirted JNAIL members taking to the microphone to list their now familiar complaints about illegal immigrants, drugs, prostitution, and gangs. But, unlike in previous meetings, this time blue-shirted supporters also lined up to thank the council and offer support and services at the proposed center. John Levin of Catholic Charities noted that his organization was committed to opening a comprehensive resource center for immigrants in Palm Beach County and would be happy to partner with the town. Corn Maya representatives offered educational services for the center. Sol Silverman gave a moving speech and voiced his concern about the portrayal of immigrants in public comments before the council. When Mike Richmond stepped up to thank council members for their decision, he asked supporters of the center in the room to stand. More than three-fourths of those in the chamber rose in support.

At the end of citizen comments, Mayor Golonka thanked the public for its input, and again noted that staff now had enough direction to go forward. For the first time since work had begun on the concept of a center, in 2001, it appeared that it could become a reality. In an e-mail to the coalition members on April 9, Jim Kuretski concluded, "It has been a heartwarming experience to witness the growing community support for the JNRC [Jupiter Neighborhood Resource Center] over the past few months. THANK YOU to everyone who has supported these efforts and helped to get us to this point."

The editorial pages of the two largest newspapers in the region gave the Town Council high marks. An April 2005 endorsement from the *Sun Sentinel* titled "Jupiter Does What's Right" credited town authorities with taking a "courageous, progressive step" and "working in some sensible measures that help to resolve related issues."[3] The editorial concluded by recommending a similar solution for the nearby town of Lake Worth, noting, "Neighborhood resource centers will not replace a comprehensive, responsible national immigration policy, which the federal government is obligated to provide. But in the interminable interim, cities like Jupiter are wise to offer a solution that makes their community more livable for all its residents." The *Palm Beach Post* concurred with an April 14 editorial endorsing the town's decision and suggesting, "What Jupiter does could become a model for Lake Worth and other South Florida municipalities where immigrants have congregated."[4] Roger Buckwalter penned another guest editorial for the *Jupiter Courier*, noting that while no response could be perfect, "Jupiter has chosen a reasonable, pragmatic step that with effort, support and, yes, luck, might work. Under these admittedly difficult circumstances, this is the best move for all Jupiter residents—today's immigrants and the children of yesterday's immigrants. It at least offers a chance for more people to realize the "American Dream.""[5]

BLOWBACK: THE FAIR THREAT

The April 5 Town Council vote and immediate positive media coverage represented a high water mark for the coalition in favor of the center. Though somewhat reluctantly, the town of Jupiter had finally taken a vote to officially support a resource center on public property—and it was receiving positive feedback from the very media sources that had long been critical. For the JNAIL members, however, the town's decision was proof that their complaints were falling on deaf ears. Days after the Town Council voted to support the resource center, John Slattery, president and founding member of JNAIL, was quoted in an article in a local newspaper as saying, "This is a greater issue than just men on the street. The issue is about illegal neighborhood activity such as drugs, crime, overcrowding, gangs and illegal labor."[6] In response to the town's decision, JNAIL again contacted representatives of the anti-immigrant organization FAIR.

The Federation for American Immigration Reform had threatened legal action as early as 2004, when the idea of the center was beginning to gain traction in Jupiter. Now that the council had voted to lend its official support, FAIR and JNAIL began to discuss the specifics of legal action against the town. Michael Hethmon, one of FAIR's attorneys, who had visited Jupiter in November 2004, made a second visit to the town on August 15, 2005.[7] In anticipation of the meeting, Slattery sent several Jupiter residents an e-mail outlining the organization's strategy, which included tapping into perceptions that immigration jeopardized American jobs: "On Monday August 15th, Michael Hethmon, the Head Attorney for Federation for American Immigration Reform (FAIR) is flying in from Washington D.C. Michael and I have meetings in the morning with the Heads of several Labor Unions. Later in the evening at 7 PM we are having another meeting at Jupiter Plantation's swimming pool pavilion. The purpose of the meeting Monday evening is to discuss in detail how FAIR and the Labor Unions are going to sue the Town of Jupiter over the Illegal Immigration & Labor problem that has developed out of control in Jupiter." Slattery went on to claim that 10 percent of Jupiter's population consisted of "Illegal Aliens," whose presence required "an enormous increase in Government expenditures." Pointing to three "International Latin Drug Gangs," he claimed that the city had witnessed "a massive increase in crime." The town's answer, he complained, "is to build an Illegal Hiring Hall, on Town property at the Tax Payer's expense, so the Illegal Aliens can go there and get work illegally without paying taxes, without paying Workers Compensation Insurance and without a Work Visa." Slattery concluded his e-mail with an explanation of FAIR's legal suit against the town.

> Because the Town's actions are completely illegal we are suing them for it. If we can't get the Town Officials to stop participating in Racketeering,

Felony Harboring, Tax Evasion and Workers Compensation Insurance Fraud then we should be able to get a Federal Judge to stop them and award damages to anyone we can prove is harmed by this.

If you or anyone you know is being harmed by this overrun of Illegal Aliens in our Town, you may want to talk to Mr. Hethmon at the meeting Monday night. FAIR is willing to sue the Town on your behalf *at FAIR's expense* if a good case can be made for you.

FYI—Latin Gang related crimes are happening every day now in Jupiter. Just this past Friday night a Mexican Coyote (a Coyote is a gang member that gets paid to transport Illegal Aliens from Mexico to our area) attacked another Mexican Illegal Alien with a Machete in the parking lot of one of the apartments on Center St. Machetes are the weapons of choice among gangs when they want to send a message. (emphasis in original)

The details of Slattery's e-mail quickly came under question in the press. A *Sun Sentinel* article noted: "[T]hey don't know how many day laborers live in Jupiter, but there has been no sharp increase in crime attributed to them. A Police Department spokeswoman also said the story of the machete attack described in the e-mail was uncorroborated. 'Wow,' Public Information Officer Sally Collins said. 'This has come back to me before that we have wild men running around with machetes on Center Street. . . . Our investigation did not show that at all.'"[8]

A September *Sun Sentinel* article captured further responses from the town. Kuretski was quoted as saying, "I think this potential lawsuit is unfortunate because I consider this organization as a hate group that misinforms the public. . . . This is a national issue. FAIR doesn't care what happens in Jupiter. They don't want to see success anywhere in the country; they want immigrants sent back home." Andy Lukasik noted that the town would continue with its plans despite the threats. According to him, "There was always a possibility of a lawsuit. But we'll have to wait and see what it says. In the meantime, unless there is some order requiring us not to open the Center, we will proceed. The threat of their lawsuit isn't going to deter us from taking actions we need to take to enhance the quality of life in these neighborhoods."[9]

As reported at the time, FAIR did hire Stewart Karlin, an attorney from Fort Lauderdale, to represent potential plaintiffs in a suit against the town. Slattery tipped his hand to reveal what grounds the plaintiffs might use in a case, telling a local reporter, "Enabling them to be in the country illegally is felony harboring. Giving them a job without paying taxes is tax evasion, and workers' comp— and done on a mass scale, it's racketeering."[10]

However, despite the media spectacle, the threatened suit never materialized. According to Jill Hanson, her contacts within the labor community played an important part in defusing the situation:

> Right after Sol died was when JNAIL was threatening to sue the town. I don't know if we found out for sure, but the head of the local electrician's union was going to fund a lawsuit. And he was somebody that Sol was very close to, but he was at that time virulently anti-immigrant even though he was an Irish immigrant himself. This was within two weeks from Sol's death. I called the person in charge of the AFL-CIO [American Federation of Labor and Congress of Industrial Organizations] lawyer's coordinating committee that I was a member of. I said to the woman in charge that this union guy was getting ready to file this lawsuit. She got in touch with the lawyers for the international union of the IBEW [International Brotherhood of Electrical Workers]. They got in touch with him and pulled him off from that.

With the lawsuit in limbo, JNAIL members became increasingly frustrated. John Slattery told reporters in September, "I've been fighting this issue for three years and I got tired of playing the political game."[11] Within a year, JNAIL would file papers of dissolution and cease to exist as a formal political entity in Jupiter. Opposition to the center, however, would continue in other forms, as the issue of the labor center continued to place Jupiter in the sights of state and national restrictionist groups.

The Waiting Game

The April 5 vote in favor of a resource center meant that the coalition of supporters was suddenly transformed from an advocacy group to an action team. In the days following the vote, Councilman Kuretski sent an e-mail out to the members of the coalition of supporters of the center, stating that there was "a tremendous amount of work that needs to be completed to enable the JNRC opening to occur." Kuretski could not have been more correct. Although supporters had hoped the center might open as early as July, a number of critical issues had to be addressed first. Resolving them would take over a year.

First, the building was under contract with the Lifesong Church, which was in the process of acquiring a new building elsewhere in town. The process took longer than expected, delaying the ultimate sale of the old building to the town. The purchase of the building was not finalized until late in 2005. Moreover, the building itself had sustained water and structural damage from hurricanes

Frances and Jeanne in 2004 and Wilma in 2005. The labor center could not open until the building was brought back up to code.

Another hurdle related to the building was political. While the town had agreed to purchase the building and use it for a labor center, it also had to approve a lease with the organizations charged with administering the center. At this juncture, Catholic Charities and Corn Maya signed a memorandum of agreement to collaborate in the daily operations of the center. This agreement involved internal negotiations between two nonprofit organizations with different boards and central missions; needless to say, such a statement had to be delicately crafted. Finally, in June 2006, the lease of the building came before the Town Council. The vote on April 5 of the previous year may have seemed like the ultimate victory to the coalition of center supporters, but the June vote on the lease made it evident that the battles were far from over. Town Manager Andy Lukasik presented the lease to the Town Council and answered questions. Once again, the mayor expressed her reservations about the project, but in the end the council approved a three-year lease agreement with Catholic Charities and Corn Maya with three votes in favor and one (Don Daniels) opposed. According to this lease agreement the town would rent the building to these two nonprofit organizations for a symbolic fee of a dollar per year.

Perhaps the most important hurdle delaying the opening of the labor center was the issue of funding. The Town Council had decided that it was going to use the Lifesong Church building for the purposes of the labor center, but it had not agreed to fund daily operations. The understanding was always that the community would have to step up and operate the center. One of the limitations of the Corn Maya pilot program in 2003 was insufficient funding for permanent staff. In order for the resource center to be successful, funding and community support to staff the labor center on a regular basis were necessities. Corn Maya applied consistently for grants and sought private donations, but the resource center would need a more consistent and secure source of start-up funds. Finally, on March 23, 2006, Andy Lukasik and Jim Kuretski received an e-mail from Tom Bila, the executive director of Catholic Charities, stating, "The Catholic Charities Board met tonight. They agreed to use the funding we have to secure/manage a labor center in addition to the Catholic Charities ancillary services." Catholic Charities had voted to use $189,000 of funds it had received from an anonymous donor to finance the center's operations for eighteen months. The money came at a critical moment, as one of the members of Corn Maya explains:

By then we knew that things had been approved, and they were conditioning the building so that we could use it. One of the requirements was that we had to pay insurance and show that we had an organization with enough money to administer the center. Some organization had to show that they had enough money to support El Sol for a period of time. Unfortunately, neither Corn Maya nor the Friends of El Sol had the funds. I don't know who contacted them exactly, but Catholic Charities was called forward to help. Someone contacted them, and they provided the up-front money to run El Sol.

By this point Town Manager Andy Lukasik was convinced that the center would open, but he was also keenly aware that the issue of funding and the role that Catholic Charities played in fulfilling that need were critical. As he candidly explained, "The mayor came around, Mike and Jill came, the contingent showing up at Council to speak up in favor of a center came, you [Steigenga] came, Sister Marta came, Jim Kuretski was 'converted,' Catholic Charities stepped up. Without their up-front money it would have never happened. I was playing chicken with them for a long time—but I thought it was going to happen no matter what!"

With the building and funding secure, the next important hurdle was creating and implementing policies and practices for the center. Coalition members set out to learn anything they could from labor centers already in operation throughout the country. Several personally traveled to gather this critical information. Mike Richmond was one of the delegates sent on the research trips. He explains:

One good thing was that when Catholic Charities came aboard, the town was sending representatives to different cities, and I had no idea what this would mean for my future involvement, but I was given the chance to go with Catholic Charities to Fort Worth and to Garland, Texas, to visit their labor centers. That was a real eye-opener, to see how two other cities were addressing similar problems. I had gone online and researched Casa de Maryland and Casa Latina in Seattle. I looked at them, talked by phone with their director. I knew right away that there were other cities that were addressing this successfully.

With knowledge of the best practices of and advice from centers around the country, the coalition set out to draft its own policies. One of the most valuable lessons coalition members gathered from their research was that in order for a

Outreach meeting with immigrant workers prior to the opening of El Sol (Courtesy of Timothy J. Steigenga)

labor center to succeed its users had to feel a sense of ownership. With this in mind, they began to reach out to the community of potential users.

Coalition members had to convince workers and contractors who were accustomed to using the informal labor market on Center Street to use the formal labor center. The open-air labor market had been a staple of Jupiter for nearly a decade, and it would take a far-reaching educational effort on the part of the coalition of supporters to move it. The coalition held a meeting with potential clients in April 2006. At this meeting information about how the center would operate and what services it would provide was disseminated to an audience of more than two hundred day laborers. The coalition also held informational sessions for contractors throughout 2005 and 2006. Employers who were used to hiring people on Center Street had to be informed about how the new hiring process would operate. The coalition held these meetings not just to inform potential users about the center but also to ask for input regarding several key issues. The hours of operation, the method for hiring workers, and other daily procedures were developed with input from interested parties, in part to ensure participation and, perhaps most important, to generate that sense of ownership on the part of the day laborers and prospective employers.

While actively seeking input from potential users and hosting several informational workshops were useful, the question remained of whether that would be enough to remove *everyone* from the informal labor market on Center Street. Cleaning up the appearance of Center Street was one of the most important goals of the center because it directly addressed one of the original quality-of-life complaints of neighborhood residents. From the beginning a no-solicitation ordinance had been on the table. The Town Council had approved a no-solicitation ordinance that would fine each individual who was found soliciting workers anywhere other than at the new labor center five hundred dollars. The ordinance would not go into effect, however, until September of 2006, on the same day that the labor center officially opened. As Andy Lukasik explains, "We knew that we couldn't just have the center. We wanted the carrot, but we knew we needed the stick as well. We had to have it. We hoped not to use it, but we knew we needed to have it." By actively informing the community about the "carrot," officials greatly reduced the chances that they would ever need to resort to the "stick." Although some residents wanted the town to start enforcing the new law immediately, the council refused. "We could not implement it," explained Lukasik, "until we had somewhere for the laborers to go." To date the town has never had to levy any fines for violation of the no-solicitation ordinance.

The coalition had been hard at work for months—some individual members for years. While there were still many technical and institutional hurdles to overcome, there were also some important symbolic victories. On Saturday, August 6, 2005, Jupiter and Jacaltenango signed an official agreement to become sister cities. The mayor of Jacaltenango flew to Jupiter, where he and Karen Golonka met at Saint Peter Catholic Church. The Guatemalan foreign minister joined them to sign the official agreement. At the event each mayor gave a brief speech about what the sister city agreement meant for their communities.

A *Palm Beach Post* article quoted Jupiter's mayor, Karen Golonka, as saying, "I hope this agreement will promote a better understanding between the cultures and the towns. . . . I hope it will also bring down barriers."[12] Following the signing of the agreement, there was a dinner attended by representatives of the Guatemalan government, members of Corn Maya, and the mayor of Jacaltenango. Mayor Golonka also attended this dinner, and while the Guatemalan officials were called to another meeting, Golonka stayed for a long while, getting to know members of Corn Maya on a personal level for the first time. When asked how this meeting impacted her, she responded, "People are always

Mayors Moisés Pérez of Jacaltenango, Guatemala, and Karen Golonka of Jupiter, Florida, sign a sister city agreement, 2005 (Courtesy of Timothy J. Steigenga)

so interesting, learning about them, because of their backgrounds. Just to be able to understand the struggles . . . people are fascinating. . . . Yes, I guess the meeting did make a difference. The Guatemalan people, they just seemed nice. Maybe everybody should meet one Guatemalan person and hear their story."

THE CENTER OPENS

Finally, by the fall of 2006 all the pieces had been put in place. Catholic Charities formally committed the funding to run the center's operations for one year; the building was purchased by the town and brought up to code; day laborers and employers were informed about the labor center and their input had been taken into consideration to ensure their support; and the no-solicitation ordinance was ready to be passed by the council and enforced, further ensuring that day laborers would stop using Center Street. With all these hurdles behind them, the coalition of El Sol supporters was geared up for the grand opening of El Sol, Jupiter's Neighborhood Resource Center.

On June 2, 2006, Bishop Gerald Barbarito of the Diocese of Palm Beach came to El Sol to dedicate the building. Hundreds of local immigrants, town representatives, and El Sol supporters attended the ceremony. A *Palm Beach Post* editorial deemed the event "Blessed, and Welcome."[13] The *Jupiter Courier* ran an editorial titled "High Hopes for El Sol success," which quoted Janice Fine, an expert on workers' centers, as saying that trust "is at the core of a successful operation and the trust comes from both directions. Workers must understand and support the way the Center is operated, and there must be cooperation from local government, police, businesses and a strong grassroots organization."[14] El Sol had successfully put these key elements in place.

By the end of July, volunteers and Catholic Charities employees had registered more than 350 workers. In August, Catholic Charities hosted a "soft opening" to get both employers and workers acclimated to the location and procedures of the center. On the following Saturday, Jim Kuretski was at the El Sol building when a representative from another city's labor center stopped by for an informal tour. Kuretski explains, "Early on, I will never forget really looking up to this community that had opened a center almost ten years ago. . . . Somebody introduced me to this person, and this person remarked how we were already ahead of them in X, Y, and Z. We hadn't even officially opened yet, but it made me feel good."

Center Street, Jupiter, 2012 (Courtesy of Sandra Lazo de la Vega and Timothy J. Steigenga)

The formal opening, however, would not come until September when the no-solicitation ordinance went into effect. Since Mike Richmond was on a family vacation, volunteer Lee McCarthy was in charge of opening the building that first day. Lee and others worried that protesters could show up and create trouble, and a plainclothes officer was on hand just in case. However, no disruptions occurred, and the center simply went about its business.

El Sol organizers were also concerned that some workers might refuse to leave Center Street. What actually happened surprised even the center's most staunch supporters. On the day the center opened and the no-solicitation ordinance went into effect, Andy Lukasik drove to Center Street with the chief of police. As he describes the scene: "I still remember the first day that the solicitation ordinance went into effect and El Sol was officially opened. I still remember driving out there [to Center Street]. I didn't even believe it was the same street. It was empty. Before I could drive over there and see four to five hundred people within a two- to three-block span just standing there. Now there was nothing, absolutely nothing. That took me by surprise. In my wildest dreams I never expected that. That was our first major success. It had to be starkly evident to residents."

Stunned, he phoned Kuretski, who asked if they had gone to El Sol yet. Lukasik and the police chief then drove to the newly opened center. Virtually every day laborer and contractor in town was there. Trust, explains Kuretski, was the key ingredient responsible for the center's success.

> The law had passed at ten o'clock the night before, and 250 guys were in El Sol! In a building next to the police station! Is that trust or what? If somebody else was trying to emulate this model, they have to understand that it just doesn't happen without trust. If Corn Maya hadn't been involved, if Sister Marta hadn't been involved. . . . The trust is such an important thing. It just happened that quickly. The whole thing was founded upon trust that had been built and faith, and I don't mean that as in religious faith. To this day I remember agonizing about whether INS would show up or not, and nobody could say anything with certainty.

Over time, El Sol would come to gain the same sort of trust among the many employers who came to use its services and the community at large. With clear endorsements from Construction and Craft Workers Local 1652 of the Laborers International Union of North America, the North Palm Beach County Chamber of Commerce, and all the major regional and local newspapers, El Sol was on its way to becoming one of the most prominent and trusted nonprofit service agencies in the region.

Early approval came from some surprising quarters. On September 19 (just two weeks after the center opened), Kuretski received an e-mail from one of the original JNAIL members saying it was a pleasure now to walk on Center Street. "I believe the Council made an excellent decision creating a labor center," the writer observed. "This might be [the] next example [of] how other towns might correct their problems. Thank you for a difficult decision that has turned out excellent."

4

El Sol in the Sunshine State

I am Ramón Barreno
I am Guatemalan and I came to the United States
Searching for a better life for my family
Although leaving them caused me pain
Into this sacrifice I put all my love.
When I first came
They asked me my name
And timidly I said I did not understand.
My life was my school
Without walls or chalkboard.
This is my first school
With excellent teachers
And here I am learning
To read and write English
And I want to thank
All people who have helped me.
I will always keep them in my thoughts
And I want to say thank you very much
From the bottom of my heart.

—"Appreciation," poem written by Ramón Barreno about El Sol

Ramón Barreno read his poem "Appreciation" at the spring semester's English as a second language (ESL) graduation ceremony at El Sol. When he first came to Jupiter, Ramón could not read or write in Spanish or English. But with the help of El Sol's literacy program, he has made significant progress in developing literacy in both languages. As El Sol developed its ESL programs, it quickly became clear that a major barrier to learning English for a significant portion (15 percent or more) of the client population was a lack of basic literacy in Spanish. In response, El Sol created a general literacy program to address the needs of this population. Ramón is one of the more than one hundred students who have enrolled in this program to date.

The general literacy program is an example of the innovative and flexible programs and policies that have evolved at El Sol since it opened its doors amid protest in 2006. In the years that followed, the center would gradually gain local support, as many of its early detractors began to witness its positive influence on the community. On a typical day 100 to 150 workers use the center. El Sol is generally bustling with activity, as dozens of volunteers and the three full-time and two part-time employees juggle job placement, worker training, language classes, computer classes, kitchen responsibilities, and numerous other services and programs. A brief overview of the daily routine at El Sol provides a window into the full array of integration and social services the center offers.

A DAY AT EL SOL

El Sol's primary daily task is worker placement. When potential employers enter they are greeted by one of El Sol's volunteers at the employers' desk. The volunteer asks for some simple information: what kind of help the individual needs, how many people, for how long, and so on. In order to hire a day laborer, each potential employer must register: the process is easy, and the information necessary for registration is basic. Once the potential employer has registered, the volunteer can process the request. A customized software program (designed by one of the volunteers) matches the needs of the employer with the skills of the registered workers who are present on that day. The software communicates the request to the staff member in charge of the labor desk, who calls for the chosen worker over a public address system. Wages are agreed on between the employer and the worker depending on the type and duration of the job, with average wages running between eight and twelve dollars per hour. This process takes place at El Sol between three hundred and nine hundred times each month.

From the beginning, El Sol was designed to serve Jupiter residents, so to register at El Sol, workers must show that they reside within the town limits. In setting this policy the founders of El Sol were responding to concerns that the center would attract day laborers from other communities. As Andy Lukasik explains, "The big requirement that we had was that the center had to be geared toward folks living in Jupiter. Regardless of documentation, as long as someone could prove that they lived in the Jupiter area: that's who we're serving. It was in response to the 'if you build it, they will come' argument."

Following the town's directive, El Sol has a system in place that ensures that those who use its services are residents of Jupiter. Jocelyn Skolnik, the director of El Sol, explains the system: "Anybody who wants to use El Sol has to register

Wilberto Luna, labor coordinator, at his desk in El Sol, 2012 (Courtesy of Sandra Lazo de la Vega)

with us so that they are part of our systemized database. As part of our lease with the town, you have to reside in Jupiter to use our services. So you have to come and show a picture ID and proof that you live here in Jupiter. You register; you get an [El Sol] ID. With that ID you come in to look for work." The Jupiter residency requirement has worked well. As Lukasik pointed out, the "if you build it, they will come" fear has not come to fruition. More than seven thousand Jupiter residents have been paired with employers through El Sol each year.

While the labor program for Jupiter residents is the cornerstone of El Sol, several other programs run parallel to it every day. In the morning, coffee is served along with donated bread and pastries from local businesses. As workers wait for employers, there are a number of educational and vocational workshops under way. Every day the classrooms on the second floor of the El Sol building are filled with ESL students, and a line of workers eager to be a part of that day's computer class forms outside the computer lab in the first floor. Like the software program, the computers, network, and systems are maintained by volunteers. All the computers in the center, including those used by staff and volunteers, are donated by local universities and schools.

Waiting for work inside El Sol, 2012 (Courtesy of Sandra Lazo de la Vega)

Around noon volunteers begin to serve the second meal of the day, and an orderly line forms outside the kitchen as workers wait for their meal. For the most part, the lunches are made with food donated by local restaurants and supplemented according to the taste of the day's volunteer kitchen crew. A collection is taken among the workers to defray the cost of utensils and paper items. El Sol client and volunteer Ariel Fernando Brites joked with us about mealtime at El Sol.

> For lunch they have rice with chicken, and chicken with rice, rice con chicken, chicken *con arroz*, and *arroz con pollo* . . . stuff like that . . . and bread! Lots of bread! There is bread all over the place. Here you can have bread coming out of your nose, coming out of your ears! The bread is good. The rice with chicken is also good. The chicken with rice is rice-a-litious! It is fantastic. From time to time they do have different things. They have pastas and salad . . . always salad to make it healthy. You know we have to eat healthy!

Since most employment requests come in before noon, lunchtime is bittersweet for those who are still at the Center. After lunch the activity in El Sol's labor program begins to decrease. On an average day, approximately 25 percent of the men and women who wait at El Sol are hired. Some of the workers who were not hired that day begin to pick up the chairs and clean the floor. Those who were selected to clean become the *pendientes* for the next day, which means that their names are placed on a preferential list so they will be the first ones to go out for work. El Sol's labor program ends at 2:30 p.m. on most days, but the activity inside the center continues well into the evening. After the labor program ends for the day, a number of educational programs, including the evening English classes, swing into action. El Sol is currently home to an astounding fourteen different educational and outreach programs serving over two thousand registered workers.

El Sol's Programs

Even prior to the opening of El Sol, it was clear that there was a huge unmet need for legal services among the immigrant community in Jupiter. Within the first year of operation, El Sol opened a Legal Clinic to provide workers with assistance in dealing with wage theft, immigration, and other miscellaneous cases. Board member and volunteer attorney Jill Hanson tells the story of one of the early cases she addressed at El Sol. A local golf course had summarily fired a group of workers in violation of the National Labor Relations Act. Hanson explains how they came to the center desperate for help.

> I was here early in the morning. I was going to train a new Spanish-speaking volunteer on how to do the employer desk. So about 6:30 a.m. this whole group of guys came in. They said, "Antonio said we could get help here." Fortunately the Spanish-speaking volunteer was there because at that time I did not speak any Spanish, so she translated for me. What had happened was that they had gotten a new supervisor. The new supervisor had changed the rules. It used to be that they worked five and a half days. Saturdays they worked from 6 a.m. until 10 a.m. Many of them had other jobs after that. What had happened with this new supervisor is that it had rained on Friday and he said that they had to work all day Saturday to make up for the rain. They had never had to do that before. As a group they said that they were not going to do it. As a labor lawyer, I knew about the National Labor Relations Act. They had gotten together to basically make a protest about their working conditions.

Hanson was moved to action by what she heard and became an advocate for the men who had been fired. She was able to negotiate a favorable outcome for the workers.

> I called the manager of the golf club. They got their lawyer on the phone. I think this was on July Fourth weekend, 2007. The lawyer ultimately asked that if they put them back to work by Thursday, if that would be OK. It was very tense because we didn't know if they were going to call immigration and have them picked up. So I went up there. . . . We met in a park, and they were supposed to give their answer about whether they would go back to work or not. The security guy with the golf club drove over there to get the answer. He said to me that these guys needed a union. He said to me that they were great workers and that it was terrible what happened to them. From that I had a sense that they were legitimate about making the offer for the guys to go back to work. They did go back to work, and some of them are still working there.

As far as the workers were concerned, Hanson had performed a miracle: helping them return to their jobs without filing a lawsuit. Surely without El Sol the workers would not have known who to turn to for support. In appreciation, the workers who were reinstated at the golf club wrote a ballad, or *corrido*, titled "El Regreso" (The Return), dramatizing the event.

Amigos con su permiso	Friends, with your permission
Voy a cantar un corrido.	I will sing a *corrido*
De lo que pasó en un pueblo	of something that happened in a town
De los Estados Unidos.	in the United States.
A muchos trabajadores	Many workers
Ya los habían despedido.	had already been fired.
Fue un sábado en la mañana	It was a Saturday morning.
Nadie se lo imaginaba,	Nobody could have imagined it.
Todos iban al trabajo	Everyone went to work
Como todos los días.	like they did every day.
Pero ese día, el patrón	But that day, the boss
A todos los despedía.	fired everyone.
Le dice el Galo al Felipe,	Galo asked Felipe,
¿Ahora qué vamos a hacer?	"What will we do now?

Si nos cruzamos de brazos	If we cross our arms
Todos vamos a perder.	we will all lose."
Hay unos que se quedaron	Some of them stayed
Pues que le vamos a hacer.	but what can we do?
No los quiero mencionar	I do not want to mention them
Porque no vale la pena;	because it is not worth it.
Decían que eran valientes	They said they were brave
Pero no van a la guerra	but they do not go to war.
Ustedes ya saben quién son	You know who you are.
Allá Dios sí los condena.	God will condemn them.
Voy a decirles un consejo,	I will give you some advice;
No importa de donde son	it does not matter where you are from.
Si un día tienen problemas	If someday you have problems
Vayan a la casa del Sol	go to the house of Sol.
Allí les brindan ayuda	There, they will help you
Sin ninguna condición.	without any conditions.
El Señor Sol ya se fue	Mr. Sol has already gone.
Ahora ya está descansando.	Now he is resting.
Sola quedó su mujer,	His wife was left alone
Pero sigue trabajando.	but she is still working,
Con ayuda de otras gentes	with the help of other people
Para ayudar al hispano.	to help Hispanics.
Ya con esta me despido	With this I bid you goodbye.
Ya terminé de cantar.	I have finished singing.
Lo que le acabo de hablar	What I have just spoken
Fue la purita verdad.	was the pure truth.

El Sol's Legal Clinic now takes on more than one hundred cases a year, ranging from serious immigration issues to traffic tickets. In some cases, El Sol has assisted individuals who have the ability to regularize their immigration status but lack the knowledge or ability to pay the legal fees. Perhaps most important, the Legal Clinic provides a trusted place for individuals to come forward with their legal questions and issues. For example, a client recently came to the clinic with a formal document demanding that he appear in court. Afraid, the young man brought the document to the Legal Clinic to have it explained. It turned out that he had been a witness to a crime and had reported it, and the document was simply requesting his presence in court to verify his testimony. Without the Legal Clinic, he would likely have ignored the request and his testimony would not have been used in the case.

Soon after El Sol opened, volunteers also identified a need for health care and formed a Health Committee to coordinate these services. While focusing on preventive care, such as immunizations and screenings, the Health Committee also provides medical referrals for patients with serious health care needs. During an early health screening, for instance, a forty-one-year-old named Jesús tested poorly for eyesight. He had been unable to see well since childhood but had never been able to identify the problem. The El Sol Health Committee was able to arrange for a more complete eye exam and subsequent treatment for what Jesús found out were cataracts in both eyes. The committee identified a doctor who was willing to operate on him at no cost. After the operations, Jesús was able to see clearly for the first time in his life. El Sol provides such health-related referrals to hundreds of patients a year.

A more quotidian need addressed by El Sol comes in the form of daily meals. The food program at El Sol serves two meals a day, seven days a week. Like many of the programs at El Sol, this one also started relatively small and grew to meet the needs of the community. All the food that is served through this program is donated by the community and cooked by all-volunteer crews. On a typical day El Sol serves about seventy meals on a shoestring budget. Kitchen coordinator Andi Cleveland describes the creativity, resourcefulness, and sometimes sheer good luck of the volunteer crews: "I remember one day walking into the kitchen a couple of years ago and there wasn't anything really to cook with. Ten minutes later a woman walked in with trays of food left over from a wedding her family had that previous weekend. It was enough food that day so no one went away hungry."

Food donations arrive daily, a strong testament to community support for El Sol. Several local businesses donate on a regular basis, including grocery stores, restaurants, and coffee shops. Individual Jupiter residents also donate regularly. Since the first day El Sol opened, donations of bread, rice, beans, and other staple food items have come in from community residents. Local churches have also donated generously to the kitchen program. Through a combination of contacts coming from kitchen volunteers and local churches, El Sol boasts a new range, freezer, sink, and countertops in the fully operational kitchen, which is certified by the Health Department.

The food program at El Sol has evolved along with the needs of the Jupiter community at large. While Jupiter as a whole is a relatively affluent community, many of its residents, immigrants as well as nonimmigrants, were severely affected by the downturn in the economy in 2007–8. Prior to El Sol, the town of Jupiter had little experience with any social services. When residents began asking the town for assistance, it turned to El Sol. The relationship between El Sol and the town has become a symbiotic one: the town can rely on El Sol to address needs in the community, including the growing need for food. As El Sol's director, Jocelyn Skolnik, explains:

> We have a good relationship with the town. Anne Lyons [the assistant town manager] sent me a letter explaining that there were people who had been coming to the town . . . families who had lost their main source of income and were struggling with food. So Anne asked us if El Sol would be willing to open up a food pantry, and that's how that program started. Now we have a food pantry: we partnered with CROS [Christians Reaching Out to Society] Ministries and other agencies. It is from our productive and positive relationship with the town that if either of us identifies a need within the community, we can assess if it is within the mission of El Sol to be able to provide a service for that need, to improve the quality of life.

Thus El Sol is now also home to the only food pantry operating in northern Palm Beach County. Like all the other services that El Sol provides, the food pantry is available to all Jupiter residents. The clientele served by the food pantry (and other El Sol services) has become increasingly diverse, with more nonimmigrants coming to the center on a regular basis.

While the food program at El Sol is the engine that drives the train of volunteers who come to the center each day, it is the educational programs that serve the process of long-term integration in the community. El Sol's educational program hosts daytime and nighttime classes in English, basic literacy, computer literacy, financial literacy, vocational training, civics, and family literacy to help parents prepare their children for success in school. In an initial needs-assessment survey of the immigrant community in Jupiter (conducted in 2001, well before a resource center began to take shape) the need for English classes became clear, and students from FAU began working with Corn Maya Inc. to address this need. Skolnik, who would later become the director of El Sol, began as one of the student interns involved in the initial ESL program at the Corn Maya office. She explains her trajectory with one of her former ESL students: "One of my first students, his story is fantastic! He came to the classes; he didn't know any English. He was one of the ones who was so interested that he continued with us at FAU. . . . He came to El Sol once El Sol opened. He helped start a literacy program here now. I love teaching ESL, so after my El Sol job I still teach ESL. I teach level 6, which is the most advanced level that the school district offers, and he is my student again!" The English as a second language program at El Sol has grown along with the organization. At the December 2010 ESL graduation ceremony, Mark Mellone, an assistant principal with the school district, noted that El Sol was "a huge success and provide[d] an unbelievable opportunity to our community."[1] In a typical year the ESL program graduates between two and three hundred students to a higher level of English-language literacy.

The English classes may be the most popular part of the education program, but the program also has options for those who require basic literacy training. As Ramón's story at the beginning of this chapter illustrates, many of El Sol's clients had never learned to read or write in their native language and lacked the opportunity to attend school in their native country. Skolnik explains how the education program evolved to meet those needs.

> The community is very diverse and has so many various needs. I think that is part of the reason why we have so many programs. For example, in our English classes we had students who were simply not advancing. We were aware that there was a group of people who had never attended school; they were illiterate. They are sitting inside a class next to people who were teachers in their home countries, and they can't keep up. They haven't been in a classroom setting; they don't know how to read and write. Spanish is their second language. Here in El Sol we must have thirteen or fourteen of the twenty-three Mayan dialects. We once had an anthropologist come study how language travels. Here in our Jupiter, South Florida coastal community, you have people speaking Mam, Kakchiquel, etc. . . . ancient languages. So we know that not everybody needs it, but to address the needs of those who did we opened up an adult literacy program. People can come and learn how to read and write, do basic math, and move on until they can get their high school diploma. We have tried to address the various needs by opening programs. Obviously we won't open a program for a single individual, but if there is a need that is widespread enough we will try to provide a service to address it.

The basic literacy program that Skolnik describes was started by the workers themselves; none of the programs at El Sol would be successful if the workers were not an active part of the process. The workers are an integral part of the organization, and as such they are well organized and represented. From the beginning, representatives of El Sol began meeting with workers to create a Workers' Council. The idea was to involve the workers in rule making and advising on El Sol policy. Although the initial members of the council were appointed on a rotating basis to provide experienced candidates, it held its first election in 2008 and elected representatives from the full workers' assembly.[2] Director Skolnik explains the role and function of the Workers' Council at El Sol: "We organized the Workers' Council, which is democratically elected by everybody in the assembly. The assembly makes sure that we always keep the workers' issues in mind. They were the ones that helped make sure that we were distributing jobs fairly. For example, if an employer comes in and asks for an individual by name, then that individual goes to work. That was something that wasn't up to me. That was something that we did by consensus and with the Workers' Council. We have always followed up with concerns and made sure that those

Edmundo, former president of the Workers' Council (Courtesy of Sandra Lazo de la Vega)

get addressed." Other policy concerns that have been addressed via the Workers' Council include ensuring that workers actually have the skills they claim to possess on registration (e.g., English-language or trade-specific skills such as masonry or carpentry), patrolling outside the building to ensure that workers or employers do not bypass the formal hiring process, and imposing penalties on those who violate center rules. The president of the Workers' Council also serves as a member of the El Sol Board of Directors, and thus serves as a conduit between the workers and the formal decision-making body of the center.

The Workers' Council continues to play a critical role in the daily functioning and decision making of the El Sol center and in the lives of its members. The council derives its authority from the full assembly of workers, who elect its members and vote on major policy changes related to workers. Although no organization can be perfectly responsive to all constituencies, the Workers' Council provides an important vehicle for expressing concerns about staff responsiveness, policy issues, real or perceived injustices in the rules or operation of the center, and other day-to-day policy issues. Perhaps most important, the members of the council are charged with the responsibility of representing their coworkers and clients of the center.

COMMUNITY OUTREACH AND PARTNERSHIPS

El Sol's services and programs reach far beyond the immigrant community and seek to build bridges of communication and understanding between Jupiter's newest immigrants and longtime residents of the town. El Sol sponsors a community service program, through which immigrant workers give back to the community by participating in monthly volunteer projects such as neighborhood cleanups and working on Habitat for Humanity projects. Each year hundreds of workers from El Sol volunteer in different community service projects throughout Jupiter. In December 2010, for example, workers from El Sol volunteered to complete the installation of roof shingles and painted a home built for Habitat for Humanity. Through a partnership between Habitat for Humanity International and El Sol, workers can log their volunteer hours in Jupiter to contribute toward supplies and labor for improving their own homes in Guatemala. Thanks to the partnership between El Sol and Habitat International, three houses have been built in Guatemala so far and over three hundred families in Jupiter are at different stages of the application process. Beyond the collaboration with Habitat for Humanity, El Sol workers volunteer in numerous other projects in and around Jupiter, such as the annual Great American Clean-Up.

El Sol workers also volunteer their time each year during the Martin Luther King Jr. Day of Service. In January 2010, for instance, volunteers renovated the interior of a local nonprofit preschool that serves low-income and minority children and families in Jupiter. The El Sol crew painted and changed insulation and ceiling tiles. When they finished the job, the director of the preschool sent a letter to Jupiter's mayor, expressing her deepest appreciation and stating that thanks to the work of the El Sol crew the preschool had been able to save over five thousand dollars. That same month El Sol workers also painted a local home in Pine Gardens South. The homeowners, a woman and her disabled daughter, were having trouble doing repairs and yard work needed to keep the home up to town code standards. The workers who volunteer for these activities give up the chance to obtain a paying job at El Sol for that day. Nonetheless, El Sol workers volunteer hundreds of hours in multiple projects every year. The community services coordinator of the Solid Waste Authority (a frequent partner for El Sol projects) noted that "since the agency began partnering with El Sol . . . it has been able to double the number of people it is able to help."[3]

Each month El Sol hosts a community movie night showcasing films that touch on issues of intercultural contact, immigration, and related topics. Movie nights are free and are frequented by El Sol users and volunteers, their friends and families, and other Jupiter residents. The program includes both English- and Spanish-language movies, always with subtitles so that all in attendance can understand. At informal discussions following each film, migrants and non-migrants share their personal experiences, opinions, and reactions to the movie. Because the themes often hit close to home for those in attendance, this small event represents a great opportunity to increase the understanding between two previously disconnected segments of society in Jupiter.

Another important outreach event sponsored by El Sol is the annual Art-Fest. Andi Cleveland, one of the volunteers whose work served as the foundation for the first ArtFest, explains.

> The art program started when Betzy [another volunteer at El Sol] and
> I were working in the kitchen together. We were both volunteers there.
> We started talking about the fact that the guys didn't have anything to
> do, and they were probably really bored [while they waited for work].
> We started saying, "Wouldn't I hate that—just sitting there? Let's see if
> we can do maybe some art projects." I am not a crafty person, so I told
> Betzy I could get the supplies but she had to do the things. That's how we
> started. . . . Then we saw some of their drawings . . . [as] the guys started

bringing in some of their artwork! Wow. We thought these could sell. We started thinking about a company, and over the summer we worked with a student from Florida International University and he set up a nonprofit organization to sell some of the stuff and it became a huge thing; the Artfest spun out of that.

The ArtFest takes place each November in the El Sol building. The event is marketed to the Jupiter community as an opportunity to purchase handmade crafts in advance of the holiday season. In the months prior to the ArtFest, El Sol users make jewelry and other items to sell at the event. There are also several very talented painters who use the services of El Sol. Sunshine Artworks, the nonprofit organization formed by volunteers of El Sol, was established to support and promote the artwork of El Sol users in 2009. Lenin Cochoy of Santa Clara, Sololá, in Guatemala, is one of the most successful artists at El Sol and has sold several paintings and shown his work at local galleries. He paints in a traditional Guatemalan style, depicting scenes of everyday life in rural Guatemala. Another Guatemalan artist who has found success through El Sol is José Antonio González Chavajay of San Pedro la Laguna. His paintings also depict traditional scenes of life in Guatemala, but his most popular work showcases migration. Some of José Antonio's paintings are divided into three panels: one in Guatemala, one in Mexico, and one in Jupiter. The traditional Guatemalan paintings by José Antonio, Lenin, and other El Sol artists are now on prominent display in many homes around Jupiter. The cover image of this book was painted by Pedro Chavajay, another popular artist at El Sol.

While Sunshine Artworks was founded by El Sol volunteers, El Sol also works with several long-standing nonprofit organizations in the community. El Sol's programs and outreach have forged new links between various institutions and the immigrant community in Jupiter. As Director Skolnik explains:

We have a small budget at El Sol considering how many programs we have. We can do that because we have great partners. For example, we work with the school district to provide classes; we work with Florida Atlantic University and Palm Beach State College to make sure we have enough volunteers. We work with CROS Ministries; they operate the food pantry. That is a critical part of our organization. We are here as a catalyst. . . . El Sol becomes the connector. We have the community that trusts the center, a person or agency interested in giving the service, and we provide a space for it.

El Sol serves as a location where service agencies can make contact with a population that might be otherwise difficult to approach. The immigrants in Jupiter feel that they can trust El Sol and the agencies that work with them. Social services providers and public agencies often find immigrant communities difficult to access. El Sol bridges this divide.

Trust is an integral component of El Sol. A 2009 survey conducted at El Sol found that 93 percent of respondents felt that they were a part of the El Sol community and 92 percent felt that they were a part of the larger Jupiter community. Diego Rojas, the president of the Workers' Council, recently expressed that sense of trust and belonging in an open letter to the El Sol board. The letter reads in part:

> As president of the board of directors of the *jornaleros*, or day laborers, of EL SOL, I bring everyone a great personal greeting, both in the name of the workers, as much as in God's name. The reason for this statement is to thank you for the good welcome that you are giving to us without regard to the color of our skin, our race, our language, or our status as migrants, since we are from Spanish speaking countries. I have been thankful and been surprised by the treatment that you give us, as if we were another member of your family. Thank you, thank you very much for this approach because even in our countries we are discriminated because we are an indigenous people in a community with Hispanic pride.

The town of Jupiter frequently relies on the bonds of trust established at El Sol to reach out to the immigrants. The Police Department, for example, regularly hosts well-attended workshops pertaining to codes, bike safety, and other topics of relevance to the immigrant community. Code compliance, recycling programs, and other town outreach activities also take place on a regular basis in the El Sol building.

El Sol also relies on its partnerships with other organizations for everyday support. While many of El Sol's volunteers are individual community residents with no institutional affiliations, a significant number of volunteers and interns come from local universities. Student interns and volunteers play a particularly important role in staffing the ESL programs and providing administrative support for many of El Sol's operations. Many of the students who interned at El Sol continue to support its mission and programs, and their lives have been changed in important ways. Skolnik shares the story of one student whose participation with El Sol changed his life: "I know one of the students who gave a speech at the recent graduation was inspired by El Sol. He was at the community college; he was studying Spanish, didn't really know what he wanted to do, and when he came to El Sol and became an ESL teacher it was a revelation to him. He is now at the University of Florida and is studying to be a teacher; it is what he wants to do with his life. It gave him a purpose and a guide."

Local students at the high school level in Jupiter have also lent their support to El Sol. The Spanish Club at the local high school provides regular volunteers for ESL and other projects. In 2007, a short time after El Sol officially opened, a group of three students from Jupiter High School produced a short documentary telling the story of Jupiter and El Sol. Titled *Jupiter or Bust: The El Sol Solution*, it won the grand prize in a national contest sponsored by the television network C-SPAN. In *Jupiter or Bust*, the high school seniors interviewed the mayor, members of the Town Council, representatives of the Police Department, Jupiter residents, and El Sol volunteers. This documentary currently serves as a powerful tool for El Sol: it is an integral part of tours of the center for funding agencies, potential volunteers, and individual residents who simply want to learn more about El Sol.

Another important documentary featuring El Sol and its successes is *Brother Towns: Pueblos Hermanos*. Directed by Dr. Charles Thompson of the Center for Documentary Studies at Duke University, *Brother Towns* tells the story of Jupiter and Jacaltenango. *Brother Towns* has been screened in Jacaltenango, in Jupiter, and at several universities, churches, and film festivals. Hundreds of Jupiter residents attended the screenings in Jupiter when the film was premiered there.

Local media stories have also frequently highlighted many of El Sol's successes. Since the opening of El Sol, media coverage of the center has shifted away from the polarizing language of 2004 and 2005. In April 2005, prior to the opening of the center, an editorial in the *Sun Sentinel* titled "Jupiter Does What's Right" heralded the courage of the town, saying, "[E]very once in a while, politicians do what's right, even though it is not popular."[4] Since 2006, editorials and articles in the *Palm Beach Post*, *Jupiter Courier*, and *Sun Sentinel* have covered El Sol in a primarily positive light. One year after El Sol officially opened, an article in the *Palm Beach Post* essentially declared it to have been successful at addressing the neighborhood complaints that spurred its creation. The article, titled "Labor Center Delivers Jobs, Calmer Streets," quotes a user of El Sol's services, saying, "There's order here [at El Sol], there is respect here. Not over there [on Center Street], people would hit each other there."[5] In a similar vein, the *Jupiter Courier* published an article titled "El Sol Marks a Year of Success."[6]

In 2011 El Sol was featured in an editorial in the *New York Times* applauding Jupiter for its creative response to the issues surrounding day labor.[7]

Mike Richmond deserves significant credit for many of El Sol's early successes and positive coverage in the media. He was El Sol's first president, and prior to his involvement with El Sol he had a long career as a journalist. In the years prior to the opening of El Sol, he wrote many articles and letters to the editor in support of the center. After El Sol opened, Richmond worked tirelessly not just as its president but also as its main media point person. In Richmond's opinion, El Sol not only has been a resounding success at addressing these original issues but it has also brought a community together: "El Sol stands as a testament to the good people of Jupiter, who did not just idly stand by and look the other way or to the federal or state government to solve their problem. . . . If other towns want to see how we did it, they should come and visit El Sol."

Although many elected officials initially viewed the idea of a labor center with skepticism, the town has now embraced El Sol. Asked to provide a candid evaluation of El Sol, Town Manager Andy Lukasik was effusive in his praise: "It has exceeded our expectations. I believe it is the cast of characters that we have involved that makes the difference. It is the community, the nature of our community. . . . The center reflects the overall philosophy of the community and how we treat people. People are people, and they need to be treated with dignity and respect, regardless of where they are from and what their background is. Our community participation reflects that."

CHALLENGES, GROWING PAINS, AND "MILAGROS"

While the success of El Sol has been significant, the organization faced numerous and formidable challenges during its first years of operation. When El Sol first opened its doors, it was managed by three very different organizations: Catholic Charities, Friends of El Sol, and Corn Maya. As might be expected, differences in philosophy, management style, and mission characterized many of the early interactions at the center. Although Catholic Charities provided the staff, all volunteers were organized and coordinated through the Friends and Corn Maya. Jill Hanson describes some of early differences that arose.

> Without Catholic Charities, El Sol never would have gotten out of the minds of its supporters, and into a building. However, just after Catholic Charities stepped up to offer funding for El Sol, its local leadership changed. The charismatic leadership style of El Sol's community activists clashed

with the more bureaucratic leadership style of Catholic Charities' new administrators. El Sol's leaders just wanted to get things done; Catholic Charities leaders often seemed much more concerned about liability issues.... I'm glad to say that today, the top administrators at Catholic Charities are very sympathetic to the cause of immigrants, and in fact, we are working closely with Catholic Charities Immigration Legal Services to help them out on some immigration cases.

Catholic Charities had committed to eighteen months of running the center, but after a period of only a few months the executive director began to hint that it might withdraw its funding earlier. During the tense period of transition, Corn Maya initially served as the primary fund-raising arm until the Friends of El Sol was able to gain its own 501(c)(3) status in early 2007. While Corn Maya and the Friends drafted a memorandum of understanding outlining individual and shared collaborative responsibilities, gaining cooperation from Catholic Charities was significantly more difficult. Service contracts had to be terminated, accounts transferred, and many other details worked out. One of the biggest hurdles was gaining access to the database of employers and workers that Catholic Charities held while it ran the center. For legal reasons, it did not share that information with the other two organizations. Without the list of registered workers, Corn Maya and the Friends would have to start from scratch. This was an extremely daunting task, as volunteers and employees had compiled the list over the course of two years. Now the Friends and Corn Maya would have to re-create that list with only one employee and a group of volunteers. But as Skolnik points out, overcoming hurdles such as this one led to one of the many *milagros* (miracles) of El Sol.

One of my first tasks was to come up with a way to reregister everybody . . . everybody. I knew it was going to be difficult to say the least. I realized that they had been doing everything by hand, and I thought we needed to systematize things, make them more organized. So I thought, "You know what? This will be a fresh start." I started researching the best way to reregister everyone in a way that would allow us to have a database set up digitally so that when workers come we know who is here and we have everything in one place.

In the process of her search, Director Skolnik met Tom Choate, who would go on to be a key volunteer for El Sol. Choate worked pro bono to design sophisticated software tailor-made to suit the needs of the center—work that would otherwise have cost twenty to thirty thousand dollars.

Despite the tensions and differences in approach, the financial support of Catholic Charities was critical during the first year of operation at El Sol. When Catholic Charities made its final exit at the end of December 2007, the pieces were in place for a relatively smooth transition. Jim Kuretski noted that, although the organization was not interested in managing the center long term, it remained committed to El Sol's success: "They agreed to continue funding the center's operations, until such time that the Friends of El Sol had raised sufficient reserve funds to take over the daily operation of the center. In fact, the executive director began to provide leads to various grant opportunities for which the Friends of El Sol might qualify. Catholic Charities fulfilled a key role in helping to jump-start the El Sol center and empower our community to more effectively deal with immigrant-resident-related issues."

With Catholic Charities gone, the next major challenges for El Sol were institutionalizing the board and procuring funding. El Sol is funded entirely with grants and private donations and generates little revenue with which to sustain its operations. In the process of building the Board of Directors, the center's organizers reached out to various local leaders and religious communities for support. One of those early meetings paid major dividends when they visited the home of attorney Ed Ricci and his wife, Judge Mary Lupo. Ricci agreed to join the board and quickly proved to be among its most prolific fund-raisers. One of his former clients came to El Sol for a tour in 2007, and at the end of her tour she watched the C-SPAN film *El Sol or Bust*. Afterward she asked the organizers what they needed to make the center run, and they told her that the initial budget was well over one hundred thousand dollars. She committed to a hundred-thousand-dollar donation on the spot, and she has continued to donate regularly ever since.

Fund-raising efforts are also perpetually under way with granting agencies. The El Sol Grants Committee applies for and tracks multiple national and local grants on an annual basis. While the grants were more difficult to come by in the early years of El Sol, the organization has recently had excellent success with local foundations and has reached beyond local funders to procure significant grants from the Allegheny Franciscan Foundation and the American Cancer Society. Perhaps most important, El Sol recently met the criteria to become a sponsor for five AmeriCorps VISTA (Volunteers in Service to America) members. As the director explains, El Sol has made significant progress in targeting and institutionalizing its fund-raising process.

We have people in our community who see [that] their philanthropic interests match our needs. There is a very strong sense that perhaps they are connected to the immigrant story themselves: their ancestors or they have met immigrants. They understand that they can help that way. We have very good relationships within our community. This is a very affluent community. A lot of the gated communities provide support for the center: in funds, in volunteers, and in kind. Most of our food is donated. Every single computer here is donated, the chair you are sitting on is donated, the carpet was donated, the paint on the wall was donated, and the walls were painted by the workers in El Sol: they also give back. . . .
We also have an outstanding grant-writing committee and an experienced grant writer who has volunteered countless hours in sharing her skills with us to write effective grant proposals.

With the downturn in the economy since 2008, El Sol, like many nonprofits, has faced increasing challenges pursuing ever more scarce donations and grants. A related challenge for El Sol is to find a way to help its programs become cost neutral. The prime example of this challenge is the kitchen program. Every day El Sol workers have access to breakfast and lunch at no cost. Despite the fact that most of the food is donated and the kitchen itself is staffed by volunteers, there is still a significant cost associated with operating the kitchen. Most of this cost comes from the paper and plastic goods used to serve the food. El Sol, therefore, has a monthly deficit in this area. Recently there have been some attempts to address the issue, such as charging a minimal fee for the use of the paper plates, but the money collected does not begin to cover the full costs of the program.

Like many new organizations, El Sol has also faced growing pains as it refines its mission and programs. In the politically charged atmosphere of the national immigration debate, El Sol has come under pressure to take a particular stance or join with political immigration advocacy organizations. Just as its opponents want to utilize El Sol as a battlefront in the immigration wars, some El Sol supporters would like to see the organization play a larger role in national and state immigration reform movements. Ultimately, the Board of Directors voted to adopt a policy calling for a humane immigration policy but chose not to align El Sol with any national or state immigration reform groups. The policy seeks to avoid any potential conflict of interest for El Sol board members by prohibiting them from formally representing El Sol as spokespeople or representatives of organizations formally engaged in immigration issues.

Another ongoing area of negotiation within the organization is deciding which programs best fit the center's mission. El Sol seeks to help day laborers help themselves gain self-sufficiency so that they can become integral members of the community. While El Sol currently offers many social and charitable programs, including two free meals a day and a pantry for individuals and families in need, the Workers' Council and other El Sol board members and clients have some reservations about such programs, fearing that they might create permanent dependency in the local population. As El Sol's services have expanded it has come to attract a larger population of clients with diverse needs, some of whom have a reduced capacity for or interest in day labor. In turn some workers fear that a culture shift (from work to services) at the center will hurt the reputation of all the workers and reduce the opportunities for jobs.

The Workers' Council, the staff, and the board share in making decisions, and their respective roles have evolved over time. Currently, the majority of decisions are made by the Board of Directors, which has some members from the immigrant community but is largely made up of nonimmigrants. As Jill Hanson explains: "One of the things about the model that is key is recognizing the power of the Workers' Council and assembly and letting them know that they have this power. Otherwise they will not buy into it. I think some of the people who went to tour different centers throughout the country saw centers that didn't work the way this one works. The ones that didn't work were the ones where the workers were passive." Passing on more of the responsibilities to the Workers' Council, however, means ensuring that its members have sufficient training to assume those responsibilities. For the Workers' Council to reach its full potential at El Sol, further workshops, classes, and other resources must be available to improve language skills, knowledge of nonprofit finances, and management skills. A major obstacle for many of the members of the Workers' Council is their irregular work schedule, which limits their access to many of the resources they need to increase their effectiveness as administrators.

Because El Sol is a public-private partnership and relies on the town-owned building, it is also vulnerable to political changes and local elections. In 2007 the last person on the Town Council who had opposed the center stepped down. In the March 2008 elections, the center's most vocal local opponent, John Parsons, who ran on a platform of closing El Sol, was handily defeated by his opponent. In 2010 Jim Kuretski, Mayor Golonka, and Todd Woodraska (all center supporters) maintained their seats by wide margins. Interestingly, none of the candidates who ran against them openly opposed the center during their campaigns either—perhaps the best indication that by that point a majority of residents had come to see El Sol as a positive addition to the Jupiter community.

The most outwardly visible challenge faced by El Sol is the group of protesters who targeted the center for almost three years. In December 2007, just a few months after the opening of El Sol, the mobile Guatemalan consulate scheduled a visit to Jupiter and came to El Sol to issue Guatemalan passports and consular identifications.[8] For many Guatemalan immigrants, the mobile consulates provide the only opportunity to renew passports or to get a consular identification card. Although these documents carry no immigration-related benefits to their holders in the United States, they are critical for those who seek to return to Guatemala, as they provide a form of identification. However, the idea of passports being issued to immigrants in Jupiter angered some of those who opposed the idea of the center. Opponents of El Sol took this opportunity to launch their first post-opening offensive. Although the protest was widely advertised, and according to an article in the *Sun Sentinel* "was supposed to draw upward of 100 protesters," only 20 people showed up. In the same article, several of the protesters were interviewed—none of whom were local residents of Jupiter. The protest had been advertised statewide on the websites of anti-immigration groups, and it was primarily members of those groups who responded. With the dissolution of JNAIL, the majority of the original Jupiter residents who had opposed the center had faded from public view. Supporters of El Sol worried

Protesters outside El Sol (Courtesy of Timothy J. Steigenga)

about the planned protest, so large numbers came to the center that day to show solidarity. In the end there were far more supporters than protesters.

Despite the low turnout for that event, opponents of El Sol continued to plan protests outside of the center. El Sol's success and the fact that other Florida communities were beginning to follow its lead made it a prime target for anti-immigrant and nativist groups at the state level. For these groups El Sol represented a magnet for immigrants and symbolized the lack of enforcement of immigration laws. Floridians for Immigration Enforcement (FLIMEN), an anti-immigrant group based in Pompano, Florida (about an hour away), had appeared on the Jupiter local scene in late 2004. After the center opened, FLIMEN began to organize weekly protests outside the El Sol building each Saturday at 9:00 a.m.

Two weeks after that first post-opening protest, FLIMEN members appeared at El Sol with cameras in hand, aggressively recording and taunting day laborers, volunteers, and employers who entered the building. While taping one employer, protester David Caulkett, FLIMEN's vice president and the Florida state adviser to FAIR, provoked a confrontation that would again drag El Sol onto the pages of local and regional newspapers. The *Palm Beach Post* reported:

> Caulkett was among the protesters waving signs Saturday morning at the corner of Military Trail and Indiantown Road, where the Center is located. At one point he walked over to one of the Center's entrances and began filming a man who was walking out with day laborers he had just hired. Randell Smith wasn't sure what was going on, he said Monday. He wasn't aware of the protest. What Smith did know, however, was that he was being filmed by a man he didn't know and wanted to stop it, he said.
> About 10:45 that morning, Jupiter police arrested Smith on simple battery charges for allegedly pushing Caulkett as he filmed. Smith said Monday he wanted only to take the camera from Caulkett, and that in the process the 59-year-old protester fell.

Immediately FLIMEN posted an edited version of the video on YouTube and the FLIMEN website. The video circulated widely among anti-immigration groups and generated significant local media coverage. Fortunately for Smith, Caulkett had filmed the entire confrontation, and the full unedited version was brought into evidence during Smith's trial in March of 2008. Smith was found not guilty, as the judge noted that the prosecution had provided insufficient evidence. Furthermore, the judge went on to state that "he sensed a 'fever' spreading across the country against people of different backgrounds. But in Jupiter, he said, there appeared to be an effort to provide much-needed services for the community."[9]

Despite Smith's acquittal and the judge's supportive statements regarding El Sol's mission, the protesters carried on with their weekly protests through 2008 and 2009. On the FLIMEN website, they advertised their weekly event, asking sympathizers to "please attend, bring others and a sign." As stated by FLIMEN the focus of the protests was to:

symbolize Jupiter as representative of what is wrong with our government,
enthuse citizens to join the protests,
demand accurate reporting by the media,
document El Sol illegal hiring transactions, and
most important, demand elected officials enforce the law.[10]

In the beginning the FLIMEN protests drew a crowd of only fifteen to twenty participants each Saturday. However, one of the largest gatherings took place on March 1, 2008, when state representative Gayle Harrell decided to utilize the El Sol protest as a venue for a press conference highlighting harsh anti-immigration legislation she had sponsored in the state legislature. In a *Palm Beach Post* editorial, Dan Moffett pilloried the event, describing it as "the most flagrant example of political demagoguery this spring." House Speaker Marco Rubio, a Republican like Harrell, dismissed her actions as "political grandstanding" and said that immigration law was a matter for federal rather than state government. Her bills did not pass.

But the protests continued, leading up to FLIMEN's biggest event, scheduled for April 18, 2009. With the financial crisis in full swing, FLIMEN organized a multigroup protest and called it the Save the American Worker Rally. The rally was widely publicized by FAIR in state and national media. The press release issued by FAIR stated:

Hundreds of south Floridians will gather this Saturday to demonstrate their support for policies that prevent illegal aliens from obtaining jobs legal U.S. workers desperately need. With a statewide unemployment rate of 9.4 percent and a stagnant economy, Floridians want reduced competition for jobs from those who have no legal right to work. Rally attendees will emphasize the need for enhanced worksite enforcement, an end to day-labor centers that cater to illegal workers and unscrupulous employers, and call for the permanent reauthorization of E-Verify—the nation's worker eligibility verification program—as sound solutions to keep illegal aliens from competing for a shrinking pool of jobs.

As discussed in the introduction to this book, speakers at this event included Joyce Kaufman, a radio talk-show host based in Fort Lauderdale; Allen West, the controversial freshman representative from Florida's Twenty-Second District; and Harrell. This event drew the largest crowd of all the events held in opposition to El Sol. On the day the Save the American Worker Rally was held, El Sol workers were engaged in a previously scheduled community service project. The local newspaper ran both stories on the front page. On the top section of the front page was a photograph of protesters holding signs about the amount of money that unauthorized individuals cost Florida every year; directly below was a photograph of an El Sol worker picking up trash as part of the community service project.[11]

After reaching its high point at the rally in April of 2009, attendance at the protests dwindled over the next few months. In a small community like Jupiter, however, the weekly protests had a lasting impact on immigrants and nonimmigrants alike. Director Skolnik recounted the experience of one El Sol client.

> I was sitting in my office, and a woman with a baby—maybe a couple of months old—she came into El Sol with her stroller. She was crying, she was bawling. She made the mistake of crossing the road right when the protest was happening. She went to Walgreens across the street because she needed to buy something. She was pushing her stroller. They had followed her, they were yelling at her. They yelled at her all the way into the Walgreens. She was so embarrassed. Everybody at Walgreens kind of turned around to see what the ruckus was. She was so embarrassed. She turned around and came running back to El Sol, she was bawling, crying so hard. They were saying, "Go home! We don't want you, Illegal! Learn English!" For me it was amazing that a group of adults would do that to a person. It was one of those shocking moments. To this day I don't understand what could have gotten into somebody to think that it was OK to do that in any scenario.

While some local residents who saw the protesters showed their support by honking horns or giving a thumbs up, others were confused, disturbed, or even outraged by the signs and slogans. In fact, El Sol began receiving more donations and volunteers once the protests began, primarily from people who felt they had to do something in reaction to the protesters. Skolnik explained:

The protesters were here from the end of 2007 until maybe March of last year [2010] or so, when the elections happened. It was hard to see it. A lot of the things they said were very hurtful. A lot of the signs were very demeaning, very hateful. . . . It was great to see that on their big days the protesters had maybe 5 to 10 people standing outside and the number of volunteers here signing up with me were like 120 to 140. We would request donations, and they came in. To me that was comforting. Everybody has the right to their opinion, but it is sad that some people think that way.

With attendance and media coverage steadily decreasing, the protests became less and less frequent. Finally, after the 2010 local elections, when the full slate of center supporters was reelected, the protests came to an end. One of the greatest fears of the protesters did come to pass. Communities in Miami, Loxa-hatchee, and Lake Worth all opened resource centers modeled on El Sol. Other Florida communities have also contacted El Sol as they explore the possibility of opening similar centers in their cities. As a member of the National Day Labor Organizing Network (NDLON), El Sol has continued to share its experiences with other centers throughout the country. Its influence has also transcended borders. The Guatemalan Ministry of Foreign Affairs asked Skolnik to present the El Sol model at a meeting in Guatemala City. Officials reported that they saw El Sol not only as a vital tool for integration in the United States but also as a possible model for addressing labor needs and reintegration in Guatemala.

A May 2008 *Palm Beach Post* editorial penned by Dan Moffett captured the essence of El Sol's struggles and successes in its first years of operation.

No community in Florida has done more to reject Americans' hypocritical approach to immigration than the Americans of Jupiter. Since the El Sol Neighborhood Resource Center opened 20 months ago, the townspeople have carried on a brave, honest and practical experiment in dealing with a problem almost no one wants to touch. It took courage for the town Council to approve leasing space for the Center, and it takes courage for supporters and volunteers to keep the operation running. . . . El Sol sees [its clients] both as workers and as human beings. The practical value of the El Sol experiment is self-evident. Dozens of workers aren't flagging down vehicles on street corners looking for jobs each morning. El Sol brought structure and safety to what was messy business. Congress has failed to solve the immigration problem, but the Center has succeeded in restoring order to the streets of Jupiter. The El Sol experiment continues to surprise skeptics with its confirmation of the common decency that very different people share.[12]

The common decency Moffett highlights lies at the core of El Sol's approach to resolving local issues by working collaboratively and approaching immigration from an integrationist rather than a restrictionist perspective. In the process this approach not only provides a practical solution to local problems but also builds bridges between communities that were formerly isolated from each other. In the chapter that follows we highlight the story of one family that was formed through the center, forever changing the lives of the members of the family and the larger community of El Sol.

5

The El Sol Family

Many of the volunteers and staff members who work at El Sol have seen their lives evolve in unexpected ways as they have come to see the more human face of immigration. As El Sol's first volunteer coordinator and the person who opened the doors on the day the center was inaugurated, Lee McCarthy's story is particularly powerful in this respect. As an undergraduate, McCarthy had studied abroad in Mexico and Guatemala. She and her husband moved to Jupiter in 1989, and ten years later, when Jupiter was experiencing the construction and development boom that attracted so many immigrants, they bought a house in the newly developed Abacoa community. McCarthy's husband was diagnosed with cancer in 2004 and passed away within a year. Like many other Jupiter residents living outside the charter neighborhoods, McCarthy first learned about Jupiter's immigrants during that same time period, mostly reading in the local newspaper about the rising tensions. She had fond memories of the people in Mexico and Guatemala from her studies, and she "thought that this would be the perfect time to welcome them into our country." She began to attend the Friends of El Sol meetings in 2005, and by the time El Sol opened in 2006 she had been appointed volunteer coordinator. As soon as El Sol opened, McCarthy became a permanent and indispensable fixture at the center. Her involvement with El Sol changed the lives of many people, but none as profoundly as her own.

While McCarthy's story is unique, it illustrates the power of El Sol as a place of encounter: a place where Jupiter's residents are able to forge human connections with each other. These connections represent cross-cultural bridges that are critical to immigrant integration in the long term. McCarthy, who never had children of her own, forged a powerful personal connection with three young men at El Sol: Ulises and José (teenage cousins from the same village in Guatemala) and Isac (a young man from Mexico). Through a series of events facilitated by her role at El Sol, McCarthy and the three boys have evolved into a true family. Their story is a powerful one, and is best told in their own words. Through McCarthy's efforts, her two youngest sons (José and Isac) were able to regularize their immigration status. Because he was already eighteen, Ulises did not meet the same naturalization criteria. In-depth interviews with Ulises and McCarthy detail their story, and this chapter is told primarily from their point of view.

Arrival at El Sol

As detailed in chapter 2, Ulises arrived in Jupiter with his younger cousin José in 2008 when he was just seventeen years old, after a harrowing crossing of Mexico and the U.S. border. Ulises and José came to Jupiter because they had an uncle who already lived there. Ulises recalls his trip to Jupiter, his first impressions of his new home, and the mixture of fear and excitement that the beginning of this new phase of his life made him feel.

> We went from McAllen to Jupiter in bus. It took like a week. What a long trip! There were so many people in the bus. I have seen a map now, and it is so far! We were exhausted. When the bus got on the turnpike there were those toll plazas. There were lights that to me looked like police lights, and I got scared. The lights were just the toll plaza lights, but I didn't know. I was very scared. I told myself I made it this far, and now there is the police, and now it is all over. But it was just the turnpike, and we made it through fine. The bus was so packed. Most people who were in the bus were also immigrants. In Jupiter, they dropped us off at the McDonald's that is close to I-95. We arrived here in Jupiter at about 1:00 a.m. My uncle was there at the McDonald's with the money. We got off the bus. In my town in Guatemala most people think that in the United States all the houses are like skyscrapers, all of them . . . like New York and all that. I got to Jupiter, and the very first thing I did was look around and look for skyscrapers, but there were none! I was happy to see my uncle; we hadn't seen him in many years. From the McDonald's parking lot we went to the apartment where he lived. We slept there that night. We cleaned ourselves up, but I could not sleep. It was the anxiety, the fear. . . . I could not sleep. I was looking out the window to the parking lot. I was wondering about how life was here in the United States, how things were going to be. So, that was my first night here in Jupiter; I didn't sleep at all. I was thinking about my family, the language problems I was going to have.

The day following Ulises's arrival in Jupiter was a day of many firsts. Ulises did not know how to speak English when he arrived, and he needed assistance from fellow Guatemalans (*paisanos*) to negotiate the challenges of life in his new environment. His *paisanos* also introduced him to El Sol.

I think it was a Saturday the next day, so my uncle had to go to work. There were other *paisanos* who lived with him in the apartment, so for lunch they took us to Burger King on Military Trail. We went in, and a *paisano* told me, "OK, order what you want." Everything was in English. How was I supposed to know what to order? I knew a couple of words in English, but not enough to say "I want a number 5." So I told my *paisano* that I didn't know how to speak English, and so he ordered for us. After lunch we left, and he started talking to us about life here in Jupiter: what the work is like, what the most common jobs were that we were going to have, how American people were, some good, some bad. As we were walking out of the restaurant parking lot, he pointed out El Sol. That was the first time I saw El Sol. He said, "You see that building over there? That is El Sol. Tomorrow we will come here to look for work in this building."

In Guatemala, Ulises had heard some things about life and work in the United States, but he still felt anxious about embarking on the journey. He had to learn new things and readjust his life and expectations to fit the new circumstances in Jupiter.

In Guatemala when you go look for work, you obviously go well dressed, well groomed, with a tie and all that. I only had the clothes I had brought from Guatemala. I thought, I don't speak the language, I don't have the right clothes, and how can I go here to find work without a tie?! It had never occurred to me that to work in landscaping you didn't need a tie. So I was worried. When my uncle got home in the evening, I told him that tomorrow we were going to look for work and I had no clothes, nothing nice. He laughed. He told me that the jobs that we do we don't need ties for. He still took me to Walmart that night. He bought us some clothes; they loaned us the money to buy clothes. Little by little we paid it off. The next day we went to El Sol. The night before he prepared a backpack for us with a notebook and a pencil. He said, "This is for you." The next day he woke us up at 5:00 a.m. Of course, we didn't want to wake up. He said, "This is not Guatemala. You wanted to come to the United States, and

here you are. This is what it is. Wake up, start making breakfast. With a
full belly you can go find work." So we started cooking breakfast. I had
cooked a little bit before. My mom had taught me how to cook a little.
I used to burn everything, but I cooked. We ate breakfast, and we went
to El Sol.

Despite El Sol's primary focus on employment, finding work remains difficult when the number of day laborers far exceeds the number of people who
need their services on any given day. Recognizing this fact, El Sol also offers a
number of programs that day laborers can participate in while they wait for
work. For Ulises this was one of the main benefits of El Sol in his early days.
Like many other migrants, he struggled with English. By taking advantage of
the educational programs offered at El Sol and the local high school, Ulises per-
severed, and less than four years after his arrival he speaks English fluently.

We didn't find a job at El Sol for six months. The notebook that my uncle
had given me, though, I used that to go to the English classes at El Sol.
I knew a couple of words, but I couldn't have written a sentence. In
Guatemala they had taught me the verb *to be*, but it was something very
difficult for me. Here we started to learn English little by little, starting
with the ABCs. I went to the classes at El Sol during the daytime. At night
I signed up for the English classes at the high school with my uncle and
my cousin and the other *paisanos*. They were in level 4; I was in level 2.
I used to dream about being in level 4, it seemed like such a task. Little by
little . . . from level 2, I moved to level 2b, then level 3, and my uncle and
them were in level 4 still. They could not pass to the next level. From level
3 I finally made it to level 4 with them. It took me about one year to make
it there to level 4. They were surprised, and somewhat upset I think. I also
got stuck in level 4, though. I took it twice. Then they passed us all together
to level 5, but we got stuck there too. The exam was hard. We repeated
level 5 like three times. We finally passed and went on to level 6. I repeated
level 6 three times.

During his first months in Jupiter, Ulises was busy learning English, looking
out for his younger cousin José, and seeking work so that he could send money
back to his family in Guatemala. As is the case with the majority of day laborers
in Jupiter, Ulises lived in a *renta* with his uncle and a group of other Guatemalans.
Rentas are apartments or homes that are shared by a number of immigrants to

lower the overall cost. Over time Ulises and his cousin began to adjust to their new daily routines in Jupiter.

> We used to share a room; there were three of us in a room. We paid two hundred dollars or so per person. So we used to wake up, cook, go to El Sol to wait for work. While we waited for work, we used to go to English classes. We would come downstairs to eat lunch at El Sol. We used to wait until El Sol closed if there was no work. We would then go back to the *renta*. When it was our turn to clean, we used to clean. When it was hot we used to go play soccer, basketball, and we went to the beach sometimes. In the evenings we made dinner, and we went to classes at the high school. I read in Spanish—I had tried to read in English, but it was too hard. At the high school in our classes we did a lot of exercises, conjugating verbs and stuff like that. Anyway, so we went to the evening English classes at the high school, [then] sometimes we went home and did our homework or sometimes I read. That was a typical day.

El Sol as a Place of Encounter

By 2008, when Ulises arrived at El Sol, Lee McCarthy had already been volunteering full-time for two years. As volunteer coordinator, she was always at El Sol, giving tours to potential volunteers and organizing their schedules among hundreds of other smaller tasks. Ulises had seen McCarthy around El Sol many times before, but he vividly recalls the first time they spoke.

> One morning during English class Lee, who was the volunteer coordinator back then, walked in with some official from the university. Lee was giving this person a tour, showing her the programs and everything. So the tour finally made it to the classroom where I was learning English. The teacher stopped his lesson, and he said, "This is so and so, and she works at the university." I got very happy. I got overexcited because in Guatemala I wanted to go to medical school. Hearing that here was this person from the university made me very excited. They left our classroom and continued with their tour of El Sol. I got sad, so I left my classroom without asking my teacher. I left because I didn't want them to leave without talking to me. I went and found them. I tried to speak in English with Lee, but I stumbled on my words. Lee told me "dímelo en español." I was surprised because Lee spoke Spanish! I told her in Spanish that I wanted

to go to the university. I had no idea back then how hard it would be. How hard it was to go to the university, especially for someone in my situation. I know that there are citizens here who don't go, let alone me, *un indocumentado* [undocumented person]. Lee was surprised a little bit, I think. She smiled at me; her smile said to me, "Poor child, he doesn't know what he's talking about." So I told them I wanted to go to the university and that I wanted to speak with the representative. Lee said, "No problem. . . . Give me your name, your number, and I will speak with her and we will see what we can do." I gave her my information, and that was it. The light went out. I went back to my classroom. I didn't hear anything the next day, or the day after that.

The relationship between Ulises and McCarthy really came to be forged through Ulises's younger cousin, José. Ulises had become somewhat of a caretaker for José, but there were still many things that he could not do for him without help. Not knowing anything about how the school system works, Ulises was unable to enroll José in school on his own. McCarthy and other volunteers at El Sol represented key sources of information for Ulises and his cousin, and they facilitated the process of enrolling José in school. McCarthy remembers how she first came to find out about Ulises and José and how she became involved.

Well, it's Jim Kuretski's fault. Ulises said to one of the volunteers, "My cousin needs to be adopted." Ulises was at that time eighteen, and José was fourteen. So he said, "My cousin wants to be adopted, and he wants to go to school." So they came to me, and I was volunteer coordinator. He wanted to go to school, this was February or something, and at the end of March it happened that some friends and I went to Guatemala. I said, "Don't tell anybody we are going, [or] we will have to see everyone's family," so everybody kept their mouths shut until four days before we were going. José, Ulises, Pedro, José Antonio (they are all from the same town) all showed up at El Sol one night and got Jill and Sister Marta, and they said, "We hear you are going to Guatemala, and if you are going to be anywhere near our town . . . ," and of course, we were going to be spending a week there in San Pedro . . . so we agreed to visit their families. In San Pedro I met José's mom and Ulises's mom and dad and grandparents. José's mom said, "Oh, it's so nice to meet the mother of my son." TO ME! I didn't even know what José looked like then! I had heard about him, but I wouldn't have recognized him. He kept coming up to me after I got

back [saying] "Yo soy José!" and the next day "Yo soy José!" and I just
said, "Oh OK, aha." Persistence is everything. . . .

Well, anyway, he kept coming up to me saying he wanted to go to
school. I didn't know anything about it. I had been married thirty-five
years, no kids, never wanted kids. We had a meeting, a general El Sol
meeting, and I sat next to Jim Kuretski, and I said, "I have this kid here
who wants to go to school; he is fourteen and I don't know what to do
with him!" He said, "I know the middle school principal; I will give him a
call." So the next day I get a call to go see the principal at eleven. I went at
eleven, and the principal said, "Do you have transcripts?" and I did have
them! You talk about a bizarre situation: right before we went to Guatemala
there was a woman from Wisconsin who was down on vacation, and José's
birth mom gave her transcripts to mail when she got back to the United
States because she knew that José wanted to go to school and José couldn't
bring his transcripts with him because he swam the Rio Grande and all.
So he had these transcripts that this woman had sent from Wisconsin! So
I took them in, and they gave me the paperwork to fill out to get José in
school. So then I had to take him to the doctor, and the doctor said, "Well,
who are you? The case worker?" and I went, "Oh yes! Case worker!" And
they let me sign for things, made a copy of my driver's license. It was
amazing how it worked. I took him to get his shots, his physical. I took
him to school. I had no intention of doing any of this, and all of a sudden
I became responsible for him.

Ulises also remembers the critical role that McCarthy's trip to Guatemala
and the process of enrolling José in school played in laying the foundation for
their relationship.

It was in March that Lee, Jill, and two other people went to Guatemala
to study Spanish. They were going to San Pedro, which is about fifteen
minutes from my town, San Juan. I was chatting with one of the volunteers,
and I was telling her where I was from, and she told me that Lee and them
were going nearby. She called Lee over and put me in touch with them.
We took pictures together to send to our families. Our relationship started
that way, through the trip. They took the pictures to our families, and
being there, they became fond of our families. Our mothers of course told
them to take care of us and look out for us. They probably had no option
but to say yes. They told our moms that they would try to help us, even

though they knew that there wasn't much they could do, especially for our legal situation. They still gave our moms hope in Guatemala; they told them that they would do everything in their power to help. They came back to Jupiter, and I had picked up a job [by] then. I had a job for like fifteen days, so I didn't speak to them until fifteen days later. José, my cousin, went and spoke with Lee. He told them that he wanted to go to school. He would go every day and tell them, "I want to go to school." Poor Lee was probably fed up and said, "Fine, you will go to school!" She did us the very big favor of signing José up for school. Of course to go to school you need signatures and things, so Lee became responsible for all that.

Almost inadvertently, McCarthy had become the de facto guardian for José. Over time her relationship with José and Ulises continued to grow closer. By her own admission McCarthy had never wanted to be a mother, and she felt unprepared to open her house to teenagers, but as her relationship with the boys evolved, she opened her home to them. As McCarthy recalls, José was very persistent: "Little by little it just happened. They were living in a *renta* with eleven guys. I had said, 'I will pay your rent because you have to go to school and all, but you can't live with me. I can't have you living with me. I grew up alone; I am happy alone.' To me being alone was normal. I don't need people around me. When José came Ulises was no fool; he kind of piggybacked. Isac saw this whole thing, and he was like 'Wow—me too!' That's basically how it evolved." Ulises remembers José's persistence, too, and he also sheds light on some of the other factors that were motivating them to look for somewhere else to live.

My uncle lived here in Jupiter, but he went back to Guatemala. A couple of months before my uncle went back to Guatemala, José asked Lee if he could come live with her to her house. This was because even though our apartment was nice, it was still not that nice. People drank a lot, there were a lot of weird noises, on the weekends it was loud, and things like that. José asked Lee, and at the beginning she said no way. She said no and that she couldn't even cook anyway or anything like that. José is very persistent, though. He kept asking and asking, and Lee said, "OK, fine." So José moved in with her. I didn't want to go then. She offered me the opportunity, but at the time I didn't want to. For whatever reason, I can't remember now why, but at the time I said no when she offered me to move in with them. She was surprised at the time, but she said it was fine. We went on a trip to Atlanta for Christmas. That same Christmas my uncle went back to

Guatemala. I lived one or two more months at the *renta* after the Christmas trip, and then I went to live at Lee's house. I could not find work, and there were all the issues at the *renta*. It was also much easier because she was already taking me to the college and stuff like that. Lee used to have to go pick me up at the *renta*, take me to my classes, then she had to drop me back off at the *renta* and go back home. Lee was already involved with my life then. Our relationship was already very close. So, that's how I decided to move in with Lee and José. We started calling her "Mama," and she started calling us her *hijos* (sons). Our relationship continued to grow.

COLLEGE DREAMS

Ulises had always wanted to go to college. In Guatemala he dreamed of becoming a cardiologist, and, although he understands how difficult the circumstances are for him in the United States, he still has not lost hope. In the early days when Ulises met McCarthy, he had asked about the possibility of going to college, but she was unable to help him. Once McCarthy had become involved with José's education and had gotten to know Ulises better, she also began helping him pursue his academic goals. Today Ulises is taking a couple of classes at a time, making slow but steady progress toward his associate's degree as he continues to work to support his family in Guatemala. He recalled that McCarthy

had forgotten what I told her a long time ago, about wanting to go to the university. One day she told me that I could take classes at Palm Beach State College (PBSC) but that I had to take a test, the equivalency test or English test or something. So we went and met with the director of global education in Lake Worth in the PBSC. This program helps immigrants go to college. So we went there and [they] asked me how long I had been here, so I told her about one year. She said, I think it is best that you go back to Jupiter and study more English. Lee asked this woman how much the test cost, and it was fifteen dollars. Lee asked what the risk was, so if I took the test now, when I would be able to take it again. The director said "every week." Lee said, "Well take the exam. It doesn't cost too much, and you can take it again next week." So I took the test, and we took it to the director. I had done well. She said, "Well, you can start taking English classes here at the college." So I did. I began taking grammar, conversation, accent reduction courses, and all that. Little by little . . . after one year I took the college placement test. My English was still not sufficient. So

I continued taking English classes: three reading credits, three writing credits, and some comprehension. After that I could take Composition 1. I think this summer I will take Composition 2. So that's the story of how I made it to the college and began studying. I took math, chemistry, biology, some computer courses. I still want to be a doctor. My mom would have loved it if I had gone into the priesthood. My dad wanted me to be an architect, but I want to be a doctor, a cardiologist. I am still at the college, but it is really expensive. I take one class per semester, so it will take me forever to get the two-year diploma. I have a scholarship now through the Global Education Program, but before I used to work to pay for classes and then on top of that I had to send money to my family.

To date Ulises has been unable to adjust his immigration status, and it is unlikely that he will be able to unless some kind of immigration reform is passed. Like many other young people in his position, Ulises does everything he can, but he also is painfully aware that how far he can go is limited by his status. Even with the 2012 "Deferred Action" announcement by the Obama administration offering work authorization and a two-year reprieve from deportation for select individuals who entered the United States prior to the age of 16, the future of young people like Ulises remains uncertain. Not only is Ulises ineligible (because he entered after the age of 16) but as it stands, Deferred Action offers no path to citizenship even for those young people who do meet the specific requirements of the application process.

Building a Family

As a young child in Guatemala, Ulises's cousin José had a very difficult life. Isac, the other young man McCarthy took in, faced similar circumstances. Because they came to the United States as minors, McCarthy was able to help Isac and José adjust their immigration status. Unfortunately, because Ulises was already eighteen he was ineligible. As McCarthy explains:

I found out that the two younger boys could get papers because of a law that said that if you were under eighteen and had been abused, abandoned, or neglected you could go to family court, get a letter of dependency from the judge saying that it would be in your best interest to stay in America rather than go back to your home country. With that letter you can go to immigration and apply for your green card. We did it first with José, although he was the younger of the two who were eligible. José's mom had put him in an orphanage in Guatemala—his dad was shot to death when he was seven months old, and he lived in the woods with his mom. I saw the shed they lived in. You wouldn't put a lawnmower in it; it was awful. The orphanage that José was in was for abused, abandoned, or neglected children. So we thought, "This is textbook." Unfortunately, legal aid turned it down twice in Palm Beach because they thought it wasn't a strong enough case. But listen, you have a fourteen-year-old kid here, with no family, who was in an orphanage for abused, abandoned, or neglected children, and the case wasn't strong enough? So we heard from someone that Martin County was easier and of a lawyer in Martin County who would do it. We went up there, and they thought, "This is cut and dried." And slam dunk it was. We got it for José first and went and got him his green card. Well, as soon as José came home with his green card, all of a sudden, Isac goes like "Maybe, I could try it," but Isac is the type who doesn't get his hopes up, he just doesn't. So we were able to do it for Isac as well; unfortunately Ulises was over eighteen so it didn't matter.

After sharing so much with each other, McCarthy, José, Isac, and Ulises had become a family. McCarthy was the legal guardian of the two youngest boys, but she eventually came to fully adopt José. The decision to officially become mother and son was made jointly by José and McCarthy. She remembers fondly how they made the decision and how José became José McCarthy.

Then I told José, "I could fully adopt you or you could stay with me as legal guardian. I have gone to a lawyer, and it is basically the same thing, adopting you or being your guardian. . . . I could give the money it would cost to adopt you to your family down there." And he goes, "I want to be adopted." So I went to a lawyer here, and José decided to take "McCarthy." I said, "You don't have to do this, you really don't," but he did. I think it really helps him because he stands out. People at school remember him. "That's José McCarthy! I have always seen his name and wanted to know who that kid was!" so it won't be a bad thing. I did have him keep his whole name, though, so he is José Antonio García Chavajay McCarthy. When we went to change his Social Security card, the guy said, "You know the size of our cards, right?"

Isac chose not to be fully adopted, but he and Ulises are just as much a part of the family as José. McCarthy explains that, like all families with teenage boys, they have their differences and issues, but they make it work: "Isac was more independent; he did not take full adoption, which is fine. He is a year and a half older than José, and they are all different in their own ways. It has worked out fine, and I am very fortunate that they are great, they are smart, as well adjusted as can be, considering the circumstances, and they put up with me!"

COMPLICATIONS AT EL SOL

El Sol was the crucial place of encounter, where McCarthy, Isac, José, and Ulises forged the strong relationships that bond them as a family today. At the beginning of their relationship, however, El Sol also played a critical role in one of the first crises that they had to overcome together. McCarthy's relationship with the boys had begun to raise some issues at El Sol. Some other workers felt that her relationship with Isac, José, and Ulises meant that they had preferential access to the work opportunities at the center. Although this was not the case, the appearance of a conflict of interest began to generate gossip and complaints. Eventually, members of the board approached McCarthy about what could be done to avoid a potential conflict of interest and suggested that either she could step down or the boys might seek employment outside of the center.

As a full-time volunteer coordinator, board member, and all around "go-to" person, McCarthy was the most critical volunteer at El Sol during the early years of operation. But as her relationship with the boys evolved, she also realized that she would have to step back from her role as a volunteer in order to better fulfill her role as a mother. The issues created by the gossip at El Sol were compounded by the fact that McCarthy, who had planned for her retirement as a single woman, was now caring for three boys. She remembers how difficult it was for her to make the decision to leave her position as volunteer coordinator at El Sol, but in the end she feels the decision was the right one for her family.

> At the time the boys needed work. So I was supposed to say to them, "You stay home, I'm going to go in and work for free, but you, who need money, are not allowed to go there and wait for a job," so to me that was discriminatory against my three. So I stepped down. According to one version, some of the men there didn't want me there because I had the boys. I never got the full story. Apparently another one of the men stood up and gave some impassioned speech on my behalf. The boys all reacted kind of differently. Isac got angry, José got very sad, and Ulises was upset about it, but I can't remember very well. I told each of them separately about it. It became painfully obvious that I was going to have to go back

to work anyway. I had enough money saved for me to retire on, but . . .
I had to go back to work anyway, so things turned out the way they were
supposed to.

The controversy surrounding her new family and McCarthy's decision to
step down as volunteer coordinator affected her boys tremendously. Ulises, as
the oldest of the three, was perhaps most aware of the whole situation as it was
unfolding. From his perspective, she was forced to choose between her family
and her work at El Sol.

Well, from what I know . . . some of the workers at El Sol knew that we
were living with Lee. I think they started talking and saying things, saying
that we were being helped and whatever. The gossip made it all the way
to some of the people in charge at El Sol. These people thought it wasn't
a good situation. They thought it wasn't right; other people were jealous
because they didn't have the same opportunity we did. They told Lee that
she had to stop helping us if she wanted to continue at El Sol. Lee loved
her work at El Sol. She was there every day of the week; she opened and
closed El Sol. She said, "No, they are my sons!" She said, "Unfortunately,
these are my sons, and I can't help everyone." She said that if they didn't
want her at El Sol, she would leave. She preferred her sons. She said she
loved El Sol, but her sons came first. Lee is 100 percent mom. My opinion
about El Sol did not really change, but my opinion about some individuals
at El Sol did change.

LIFE IN THE MCCARTHY HOUSE

Having overcome this initial hurdle in the formation of their family, McCarthy
and her boys continued building their life together. Their newly formed family
settled into a hectic but comfortable routine, negotiating the everyday challenges
of family life using all the resources at their disposal, including some that are
more typical of immigrant communities. McCarthy had never really cooked
before, let alone for a family with three young men. She claims that Ulises had
the biggest appetite of the three, so she put him in charge of food. Like many
of Jupiter's migrants, Ulises had relied on a "food lady" at the *renta* before moving in with McCarthy. Food ladies are generally immigrant women who cook
traditional Guatemalan and Mexican food in large quantities in their homes
and sell full meals in the neighborhood. The McCarthy family relies on a food

lady for the majority of their meals now, but as Ulises explains, they also look forward to the weekends, when McCarthy cooks for the family.

> When I used to live at the *renta*, after a while I stopped having time to cook. I began buying food from one of the ladies who sell food. Once we moved in with Lee, she said, "I don't cook at all." We started buying dinners from the food ladies. Our breakfast was just cereal and lunch at school for José and at El Sol for me, but we needed dinner. So for dinner we bought it from the food ladies, that's how they work. I am in charge of finding us the food ladies. We change food ladies around when we get tired of the things they make. On the weekends, though, the food ladies don't cook! Lee probably felt some pressure, or maybe she just wanted to cook, I don't know, but she started cooking. I think she's a great cook, excellent. She makes great mashed potatoes and vegetables . . . her steak is great. She makes good fish, it's very good. I don't cook much anymore. . . . Now that I know she can cook, I leave it to her. She knows that I eat a whole lot. Sometimes when she cooks she complains, "Aah . . . I have to cook again." I think she says it to play around, to joke around, but I think she likes it.

McCarthy's boys are young, but they have had difficult lives already. Since becoming a family, their lives have begun to resemble the lives of American teenagers more every day. For example, like other American teenagers, cell phones are an integral part of the lives of Isac and José, so McCarthy and her boys visit the cell phone store frequently. Their family dynamic has become so comfortable that nobody at the store was aware that they are not biological family.

> I take the two younger ones into T-Mobile a lot. They have to shop every time there is a new phone out. The guy knows us already. The guy knows they're my sons, and somehow I was talking to him . . . and he said to me once how good-looking they were. He said, "Mixed are really good looking," and I guess sometimes I do say to people when they look at me with them . . . I always go like, "Oh, they look like their father," which they do. So anyway, I was saying something about calls to Mexico and Guatemala and the T-Mobile guy goes, "Wait . . . he's from Mexico and he's from Guatemala?!" He was totally confused because he just always thought that they were mine biologically and their father was from Guatemala or something.

As is evident to outside observers, McCarthy has truly become a mother to her three children. Like other families with teenagers, the McCarthy family is no stranger to the occasional dispute over curfews, chores, or other issues, but, as Ulises explains, McCarthy's love for her children is unquestionable.

Lee is my mother. I love her like I love my biological mother in Guatemala. I love her not just because of the things she has done for me. I just love her; it is a natural love. She is a great person. She is a mom through and through. She reprimands me and everything. I have the bad habit of not replacing the paper towels in the kitchen when they run out. When it runs out I don't take out the used-up roll and don't replace it with a new one. Lee hates that. . . . She gets mad. . . . "Why don't you replace it?" She walks over to the pantry where we keep the paper towels, and she counts the steps . . . one . . . two . . . three steps! She also counts her steps back and then puts in the new roll. "There it is! How hard is that?" She gets upset like that. . . . I joke around with her. She doesn't get as upset with me, more with José because of his age probably. He is sixteen; it is a difficult age. My relationship with Lee is very good. When I have homework I need help with, I ask her and she helps me. I also go to her with personal questions and issues. I tell her about my problems; she tells me her problems. I think my relationship with her is better than the other two kids . . . maybe because of my age. José and Isac are at a difficult age. I am older. She is a great person. She is so patient; if she wasn't as patient as she is I am sure all three of us would be out on the street! She is an exemplary mother. . . . She may claim she doesn't know how to cook, but she's a great mom.

OBSTACLES AND HURDLES

While McCarthy and her boys are a normal family in many respects, they confront obstacles different from those of many traditional families. For example, as difficult as it may be for a single mother to talk to her teenage boys about girls, McCarthy's talks with her boys have an added layer of complexity. In the charged environment that enveloped Jupiter and its immigrant population before the opening of El Sol, her children had heard different stories about how their status as immigrants should stop them from talking to American girls: "Isac told me once that when they lived at the *renta* one of the guys told him, 'Don't talk to American girls, they will call the police.' He was taught not to make conversation.

I said, 'Well, there's a difference between making conversation and going like "hola preciosa . . . kiss kiss kiss,"' you know? Different thing. It's not that you're not allowed to talk." McCarthy also remembers another time when the ethnic identity of her children became conflated with their social status as immigrants in Jupiter.

> It's amazing for me because I have never faced discrimination. It's been a revelation for me. Just recently, Saint Paddy's Day, I went out to a restaurant; a friend of mine was playing in an Irish band at an Irish pub. Friends I had not seen in a long time. My boys were working, and Isac and Ulises had me pick them up at their jobs to come down to the restaurant where my friends were playing. They had just gotten off their busboy jobs. We went to the bar. I knew the girl working behind the bar; she's from my husband's hometown. There were a couple of waitresses sitting around; it was towards the end of the night. So when I went in with Isac and Ulises, one of the waitresses says to the boys, "Oh, are you coming here looking for busboy jobs?" [*Laughs*] . . . I should just leave it alone, [but] I couldn't help it. I said, "Oh no, they are my sons, they're just here with me." She said, "I'm so sorry, it's just that you look like all of our busboys!" and I should have said, "Well they just got off their busboy jobs," but I just said, "It's OK, we just all look alike." Every now and then I get testy about it.

Some of the issues the family faces are simply language and cultural adjustment issues. McCarthy recounted a story about one of José's first jobs as an attendant at a fast food restaurant. The restaurant was running a special dessert promotion that required all employees to ask customers if they would like a "big dipper" with their order. José had practiced his script for taking orders and felt confident about his ability to do the job. Although his English was good, José's accent was still quite strong at this point. He was having a successful first day at work until a heavyset woman came to the counter and ordered a large quantity of menu items. After taking her order without a single mistake, José dutifully asked the woman if she would like "a big *diaper* with that order." Offended, the customer called the manager to the counter. As José squirmed, the manager explained to the customer that he had meant to say "big dipper" rather than "big diaper."

While some issues are simply cultural or language-based misunderstandings, McCarthy is also frustrated by the outright discrimination that many immigrants face in Jupiter. Her unique personal relationship with her sons has certainly made her more aware of the difficulties faced by authorized and unauthorized immigrants alike.

> Since the boys got their papers, I have been so much more relaxed. . . . But this was interesting. [One of the El Sol workers] got stopped by the sheriff. . . . He was driving on Indiantown Road, [and] made a U-turn, not illegally, but the sheriff stopped him. So he got pulled over, and they got him for driving without a license, but the reason for stopping him was that he had too much tint on his windows, one of those things. Anyway, he had to have somebody get him. He called El Sol, and Isac was there, who has a full license, and Miguel, who was working there that day too. So they go over in Miguel's car and Isac went to take the guy's truck and the cop takes Isac's license and checked him. If I had gone there to pick up that truck, he would have never looked at my license to see if I had it or if it was good, but he took Isac's and checked it to make sure it was good. Totally prejudicial.

Ulises is also particularly sensitive to the discrimination immigrants like him are subject to in Jupiter. Ulises has experienced discrimination at work, and during everyday activities such as going to the store. The protesters that targeted El Sol for a number of years also made a particularly strong impression on Ulises.

> There is a lot of discrimination in Jupiter, absolutely, sadly. Especially some people . . . some of the older people. They [the protesters] are not even from Jupiter, I don't think . . . but they have cars and they come! They drive all the way here! Sadly, there is racism in that sense. The other day I was at Walmart. Lee was waiting for me in the car; she hates going in the store, she hates shopping. So I went into Walmart because we needed a couple of things. It was nighttime. I was walking toward the car. An American woman was walking ahead of me; she was on her phone. She said to the person she was talking to on her cell, "I will call you back later because there is a Latino walking behind me." She thought I would do something to her. She said "a Latino." That happens every once in a while here in Jupiter.

The experience of migration and the issue of migration status are constantly part of life in the McCarthy household. Like most of the people who are involved with El Sol, McCarthy has come to a more nuanced understanding of the many factors that propel migrants to leave their homes in Guatemala and Mexico and come to South Florida. She is also well aware of the near impossibility of migrating through official channels for these individuals: "We say there is no such thing as an illegal human being. People who say, 'I don't mind that they are here, but they should wait and come legally.' They are unaware of the fact that they will die waiting to get here legally, that there is no way for them to do it." Although the two younger boys have adjusted their status, the migration experience continues to play an important role in their lives. As McCarthy recounted, even their childhood experiences and activities and her worries and fears as a mother are colored by their experience as migrants.

> In middle school one day, they had an "early release day." I remember José coming home from seventh grade, and instead of playing "cops and robbers" they played "immigrant and ICE." They were running through construction areas pretending it was the border, and some were chasing the others. These are kids who had just come here months before. He goes like, "Yeah mom. This is the *frontera*, and this is where ICE is." [*Laughs*] That's one way it impacts them. It kind of cracks you up. It impacted my life more than theirs, I think. I live in constant fear of them walking around, they're young kids, and being picked up for some bogus reason. They really haven't to my knowledge done anything that they should ever get picked up for, but they are kids, of course, so they think that nothing is going to happen to them or somebody they know.

As a mother McCarthy has done everything within her power to protect her children. Her two youngest now do not have to fear deportation, but her oldest lives in constant fear related to his immigration status. Ulises's status as an unauthorized immigrant severely limits the opportunities available to him. Despite the obstacles, he has not lost hope or sight of his dreams, but it has not always been easy.

> My long-term plan is going to the university, becoming a doctor. I have cardiology in mind. . . . I know for sure I want to be a doctor, but the specialty I want to study is more flexible. Maybe I will change my mind. I don't know yet. My long-term dream is to be a doctor for sure, though. For now I am working and going to college little by little. I am working on my dream one small step at a time. My life now is different from what

I would have imagined years ago. I didn't have a job for a long time. I was going to El Sol, but I wasn't taking English classes anymore. I was bored with them a little. I was going to El Sol, I would read stuff there, but then I stopped going. I was very stressed out. I stayed inside the house for a long time . . . two months or more. I didn't have a job. I was able to get out of that stage. . . . I found a little job, I started focusing more in school, I have homework, I keep myself busy. I go to El Sol, I keep myself busy; it is healthier that way.

Although Ulises is painfully aware of the difficulties that lie ahead for him, he is also keenly aware of how fortunate he is compared to other migrant workers. He derives hope from his relationship with his family, and he diligently works toward his dream of becoming a doctor.

When I arrived in Jupiter during those first couple of weeks that I could not find work I would have never imagined my life as it is now. I had school in mind, but I never imagined that I could have gone to college; I would have never expected to meet someone like Lee. I had the dream, but it was just a dream. Now, even with the tremendous difficulties ahead, I still feel it is possible. I have some more hope now. I would have never thought that I could walk around a campus like this one like today. I would have never thought that something like that would be possible because of my status. I was afraid. In my everyday life now I am not as scared as I used to be. I was more afraid when I didn't know any English. Also, I didn't know about any rights that I had. I now know . . . I know I have the right to remain silent! It is a very important right! I was so scared before when I saw the police. I used to think that they were going to arrest me and deport me. When I started learning more and I got involved with the Palm Beach Coalition for Immigrant Rights and the Florida Immigrant Coalition (FLIC) . . . I went to the "know your rights" training. Now I know more, and I feel more comfortable. I still don't have papers, but I feel more comfortable. Even so, there are some situations where people look at you like you are inferior: at school sometimes, in public places . . . things like that. I ride my bike around, but I know how to drive and I am thinking about buying a car. I know it is dangerous, but it is within my plans. I want to help my mom. She has to drive all of us around everywhere. She will explode! I want to give her a break, so maybe I will buy a car, a junker. That's in my plans, but it is still a risk, and I know that.

THE HUMAN FACE OF IMMIGRATION

While McCarthy's experience with the boys is certainly unique, it highlights the process of human interaction that goes on at El Sol every day. For many Jupiter residents who volunteer at El Sol or simply make use of its services, it is the only regular point of contact with Jupiter's immigrant community. Although many Jupiter residents remained skeptical of the newcomers even after El Sol opened, the central location on town property provides a venue where immigrant and nonimmigrant can meet and forge personal connections that have the potential to break down misconceptions and misunderstandings. As McCarthy remembers it, a man named James who hired Ulises at El Sol grew to have a personal relationship with her son that eventually made him completely change his point of view about Jupiter's immigrants.

> The man that Ulises works for, a fellow in the farms [Jupiter Farms]. He was at our first ArtFest. Ulises had told him to come to the ArtFest. The guy said, "You know, you wouldn't think an old conservative Republican like me would be here looking at this stuff, would you?" He meant it in the nicest possible way. He said, "I never would have met a Guatemalan or Mexican, not to have a conversation with," and now he's one of the biggest advocates [of El Sol]. I think if you meet people on a one-on-one basis then you realize that they're people and they have stories to tell. . . . Even when I got the boys, I didn't know their stories, and I didn't know their future plans; I didn't know Ulises wanted to be a cardiologist. So . . . even as liberal as I was, I don't think it was prejudice, but it was a perception that they just wanted to get here, send money to their families, and earn a living. Now . . . Isac wants to be an engineer and will be a good one; before he wanted to have enough money to eat. Now he's worried about his SATs [Scholastic Aptitude Test scores] and what college he will get into.

As McCarthy explains, the personal relationships she forged at El Sol were critical to her understanding of the immigrant experience. The relationships she built with her sons helped her better understand the many shades of gray in the process of migration. For people like the gentleman from Jupiter Farms whose initial views of immigrants were negative overall, El Sol provides a place where they can move beyond such abstractions and build personal relationships that open their minds to alternative perspectives.

Ulises also fondly remembers his initial conversations with his *patrón*. James made it clear to Ulises that he disapproved of immigrants and El Sol.

I started working with a guy, a Republican guy. He bought a house in Jupiter Farms, with a very large lot. He had to put in a fence, fix the yard, everything. He did it all himself. He did not go to Center Street to find someone to help him. I asked him why he didn't go look for help, and he had so many things to say: they don't speak English, they don't do what I tell them, etc. He used to be so against us before, so against. I think I had a lot to do with changing his mind. I met him at El Sol. He hired me at El Sol. He told me that he didn't like the place, that he didn't really want to come, but he needed help. He said he was just doing it as a last resort, but he said he didn't approve of El Sol. I started working with him, and little by little my relationship with him grew. One day he told me, "You know what, kids your age here in the United States, they have dreams, goals . . . what about your people? Do you guys have dreams and goals?" I told him of course I have dreams. I told him I wanted to be a cardiologist. He was very surprised. My relationship with him now is very good. I invited him to El Sol. He came to the ArtFest, and he also went to see the documentary *Brother Towns* at El Sol. I asked him what he thought of the whole thing. His opinion is very different now; his opinion about immigrants is very different.

GIVING BACK

Although certainly for Ulises his relationship with McCarthy has been the most important positive change in his life since coming to the United States, El Sol has also played a critical role in other changes. For example, Ulises today has transitioned from user to user and volunteer at El Sol. He once took full advantage of the English classes at El Sol, and today he teaches his own class. From this experience, Ulises derives a well-deserved sense of pride and accomplishment.

My life would be completely different without El Sol. I am a volunteer now at El Sol; I have made that transition. I went from user to user and volunteer. Jill Hanson gave me a ride to class once, and when she was dropping me off she told me that Kathryn Klaas [then the education coordinator at El Sol] was looking for volunteers to teach Spanish, to teach how to read and write in Spanish, for the native literacy program. She asked me if I was interested. Of course I was interested. I didn't know that there was that program. I got very happy. I got in touch with Kathryn, and she gave me two classes: one to teach how to read and one that was something like

fifth-grade-level stuff. That is how I started volunteering. I love it so
much. Later I started teaching the beginning English class. The first day
I remember I got there very early, with all my things. I was well prepared.
No tie, but prepared! I had a schedule: I would talk about this for fifteen
minutes, this other thing for another fifteen, then this and that. The first
day I was so prepared: I had copies of worksheets for the students, materials,
etc. I wrote the date on the board, but not my name. The students started
coming in. One by one they came in the classroom. When everyone was
already there, I wrote my name on the board. I saw the expression on
their faces: "What is this guy doing there?" They were probably expecting
some blond guy with light eyes, so they were surprised when I told them
I was going to be the instructor. They were so surprised. Little by little
I earned their trust. The class was great. I had nine students. It was an
excellent experience. I highly recommend it. My students would come
by after class and say "Gracias *profe*." I had never been called "*profe*"
before, so to me it was very exciting. I felt something really special when
the students called me "*profe*." I felt really big and really small at the
same time. I knew they were sincere in their thanks. I remembered when
I was in the same classroom as a student, and now I was a teacher. For
Christmas last year my students brought me gifts! It was so nice. I have
told my family in Guatemala that I am teaching English now. They are
so surprised.

As a teacher, Ulises brings his own experience into the classroom. As a migrant
himself, he can fully relate to the difficulties faced by his students in their struggle to become fluent in English.

The verb *to be* took me a very long time. It was a nightmare. Now I teach
English at El Sol. I was teaching level A, now I am teaching level B. When
I had to teach the verb *to be*, I told them, "I know how hard it will be. I
have been there." I think that it is one reason my students at El Sol come
to my class. They know that I have learned it too. Learning from someone
who has spoken it their whole life, they probably don't know all the
difficulties of learning things like that.

Ulises is clearly very thankful for the role that El Sol has played in changing
his life. He came to El Sol at a relatively young age, and the center played a critical role in shaping his experience. El Sol has provided Ulises with some of the

core elements of a home that are missing from many young migrants' lives: a set of clear rules and a place to feel safe and cared for. As Ulises explains:

El Sol is my house. It is my house; they educate us there, they feed us, they tell us when we are doing wrong. El Sol has been a home. I learned English there; they fed me. The nicest people are at El Sol. The volunteers are so nice; they opened their doors for me. El Sol has changed my life a lot . . . not just my life, but the life of many people. We have computer classes, English classes, legal assistance, all free. El Sol is a magic place, much better than Disney. I haven't been to Disneyland, but El Sol is better. I am so thankful to the volunteers. These people are so nice: they come in, they make food for us; they come in to share their time teaching us English or whatever. There are so many programs at El Sol. I have heard from many other people at El Sol who have received so much help. El Sol has grown so much since my first day with the tickets.[1] El Sol has a computerized system now. The evolution of El Sol has been amazing. If I had arrived to Jupiter that day, turned around, and there had been no El Sol, I would have still had the desire to go to college and things like that, but I would have never met Lee. Without Lee's help I don't think I would be doing all the things I am doing now. I would have never met all the nice people I have met. Without El Sol I wouldn't have had a place to improve my English, to practice. At the high school we just went there, went to class and that was it. At El Sol I was able to practice with the volunteers. I helped in the kitchen so I could practice more.

El Sol has obviously played an important role for Ulises and his adopted brothers, but in a broader sense, it also plays a critical role in the larger process of immigrant integration in the entire community of Jupiter. El Sol's most important contribution to Jupiter as a community may be yet to come. For Jupiter, El Sol represents the first step in making its immigrant population feel welcome, which is a critical component of true integration and assimilation in any community. One of the most consistent findings in academic studies of immigrant assimilation is that immigrants who do not feel welcome in their communities are the most likely ones to pursue negative behaviors such as involvement in gangs, drugs, and other elements of what sociologists have called "downward assimilation."[2] But when the community reaches out and provides new immigrants with opportunities for integration, they are much more likely to embrace those opportunities. Ulises not only has found a family in Jupiter with McCarthy and his brothers but he has also become an integral part of the larger El Sol family: "I feel so safe at El Sol, 100 percent. I feel welcome at El Sol. I feel welcome in Jupiter because of El Sol. Beyond the work the volunteers do . . . the town was also supportive. They did a great work. In the building of El Sol, inside, I feel like I am at home. I know so many people there . . . [and] the volunteers are my good friends. I say hi, we hug; it is a great family. I am very comfortable there."

6

Local Solutions and Implications for the National Immigration Debate

> Communities can't solve the immigration issue . . . they can't solve it.
> It's about managing the impacts. You're never going to solve it. Any
> community that thinks that it is going to solve the immigration issue is
> just kidding itself. Our approach was to restore and maintain quality of
> life. We wanted to restore Jupiter to be the type of community that it
> should be for all the people who live here.
>
> —ANDY LUKASIK, Jupiter town manager

The factors that made immigration an issue in Jupiter extend far beyond the control of local government. Across the United States in the so-called new destinations of Latino immigration, similar dramas are playing out in local communities. In many of those communities, day labor is the focal point of frequently rancorous debates about legal and illegal immigration. Many of the characters, statements, and debates detailed in this book could easily be transplanted to other communities with simple changes of names and places. Jupiter's experience is instructive because it raises themes that help us better understand the structural forces that generate community tensions and concerns and the manner in which those concerns are often distorted when framed in terms of the polemical national immigration debate and the plausibility of practical integrative local policy for managing these issues. Perhaps most important, the El Sol experiment in Jupiter demonstrates that the overheated rhetoric of the national immigration debate presents a series of primarily false dilemmas to local policy makers and advocates on both sides of the debate. Beginning to manage the actual day-to-day issues that arise in new destinations for immigrants leads to important insights about potential paths forward in the national immigration debate.

There is a desperate need for a rational and productive discussion about immigration at the national level in the United States. Despite current high unemployment rates in the United States, there are structural demands for immigration baked into the American sociodemographic cake. Higher education rates among the native born combined with an aging workforce (including the impending retirement of the baby boomers) have created a gap between the supply and demand for labor in the service and other sectors of the American economy. According to most estimates, the annual demand for foreign workers in the United States remains close to 1.5 million workers despite the recent economic downturn. The available number of visas, however, is closer to 1 million.[1] Any rational immigration policy must take this visa gap into account. Along with the complex set of push-and-pull factors we described in chapter 2, this gap creates a major set of incentives fueling unauthorized immigration.

Although the rhetoric surrounding unauthorized immigration is frequently bombastic and misleading, the issue is a serious one for our country. Approximately eleven million unauthorized individuals live in the United States today, representing slightly less than one-third of all the immigrants in the country. In Florida the unauthorized make up at least 10 percent of the workforce.[2] The unauthorized are firmly rooted in our communities, many of them with children or other family members who are U.S. citizens (as in the McCarthy family). These families face daunting hurdles to their successful integration into American society, as they earn less, have less job security, less access to health insurance, and worse outcomes in terms of educational attainment and earning potential than other immigrants. In simple terms, unauthorized immigration is a real threat to the United States primarily because it represents a huge obstacle to the highly effective process of immigrant integration that has prevailed throughout our history.

Threat is an important term in the immigration debate. Historically in the United States, each new wave of immigrants has been viewed as a threat by the native born. Today's immigrants are no exception. But unlike the situation prior to the 1920s, immigration today also includes the question of legality, which multiplies fears among the native born and heightens the hurdles to integration for newcomers. While the positions of nativist groups such as FAIR and FLIMEN only appeal to a small portion of the U.S. population, deep fears about immigration continue to infuse the viewpoints of the majority of U.S. voters. Many fear that immigrants (particularly the unauthorized) come to the United States to gain access to government services and compete for jobs. These fears frequently are combined with a general sense that the unauthorized are inveterate "rule breakers" who might therefore be apt to break other laws. There is also a widely held misperception that today's immigrants simply do not want to integrate into American society.

In combination with the strident positions of restrictionists, these fears and concerns make it almost impossible for federal policy makers to engage in a rational and constructive debate on immigration policy. Threats and fears about immigration are also frequently compounded in media portrayals, further polarizing the issue at the national level and increasing the trend toward policy impasse. With the failure of President Bush's 2006 and 2007 attempts at comprehensive immigration reform and the more recent defeat of the Development, Relief, and Education for Alien Minors Act (better known as the DREAM Act) under President Obama, it seems clear that something will have to change fundamentally to move the national debate in any practical direction. It may be that such change is only possible community by community, as local governments and organizations find ways to reduce the sense of threat and fear by providing the sort of human contact that comes via integrative policies such as Jupiter's El Sol Neighborhood Resource Center.

Jupiter's progress since 2006 has been remarkable. Although the process of integration will only take place over time, Jupiter's immigrant community now has a clear bridge that serves as a critical tool of the integration process. Although the long-term impact of Jupiter's choice to pursue integration cannot yet be calculated, an instructive comparison can be made between the Jupiter case and those of communities across the United States facing similar problems that enacted harsh enforcement policies intended to deflect immigrants to other communities. Hazleton (Pennsylvania), Prince William County (Virginia), and Riverside (New Jersey) represent examples of the dozens of such communities that have passed local immigration enforcement legislation in the past few years. In July 2006, as Jupiter was preparing to open El Sol, Hazleton enacted the Illegal Immigration Reform Act Ordinance. Following Hazleton's lead, Riverside passed a similar ordinance aimed at unauthorized workers. One year later, in July 2007, Prince William County adopted similar measures. In all three cases the results compare unfavorably with even the short-term outcomes in Jupiter.

An Expensive Alternative

The Hazleton Illegal Immigration Relief Act Ordinance was one of several pieces of local legislation intended to "crack down on illegal aliens" and thereby save money and improve the quality of life in the town. As was the case in Jupiter, residents of Hazleton were frustrated with the lack of interest on the part of immigration authorities when they contacted them with complaints. Hazleton instituted fines of one hundred dollars a day for landlords who rented property to individuals who could not produce Social Security cards or other forms of identification. Businesses risked losing their local commercial licenses if they hired an unauthorized worker and were also charged with checking the immigration status of all subcontractors. The ordinance required that all government business be conducted in English. Soon after enacting the original versions of the immigration-related ordinances, and under pressure from several groups questioning the constitutionality of the new laws, Hazleton had to begin scaling back. The scaled-back versions of the ordinance were still discriminatory, however, and suits soon followed. The Hazleton ordinances were successfully challenged in court at the district and appellate levels and never went into effect. Although the recent Supreme Court ruling on Arizona's SB1070 means that portions of Hazleton's laws may be reconsidered (as the court ruled that employer sanctions do not preempt federal immigration authority), other portions of the law are still being challenged on the grounds that they violate due process and Pennsylvania state laws. Estimates of the amount of money that Hazleton has already spent and will continue to spend defending what is left of its ordinances in court range from $2.8 to $5 million.[3]

The Illegal Immigration Relief Act in Riverside, New Jersey, was very similar to Hazleton's ordinance, and has had similarly costly results. The Riverside ordinance included fines of between one and two thousand dollars for landlords "harboring illegal aliens," revocation of business licenses for businesses that were found to hire unauthorized workers, and even potential jail sentences. Riverside's ordinance went even further, saying that any businesses in the United States (not just in Riverside) that "aided and abetted" the unauthorized were to be subject to penalties. Riverside faced legal challenges almost immediately after passing its immigration ordinance. Within a year it rescinded the ordinance, but by then the small town of less than ten thousand residents had already spent more than eighty thousand dollars in legal fees.[4] The cost to Riverside went well beyond the legal fees. The Riverside Coalition of Business Owners and Landlords estimates that 75 percent of the immigrants left the town and 45 percent of local businesses closed as a consequence.

Virginia's Prince William County did not rescind its immigration ordinance, but it did scale it back significantly after facing threats of legal action and opposition from within, especially from its own police chief, Charlie T. Deane. In 2008 an immigration resolution passed the County Commission that required the police to cross-list the immigration status of anybody who was stopped for a traffic violation if the officer had reason to believe that he or she was an unauthorized immigrant. The police chief realized how difficult and costly it would be to enforce such a resolution and refused to do so unless there was special training for police and special cameras were mounted on police cars. Chief Deane also protested the measure's potential to create an irreparable rift between the police department and the Latino community. The chief submitted a report to the county estimating the cost of enforcing the resolution at more than three million dollars.

Prince William County amended its resolution in April 2008 to reflect these concerns, scaling it back significantly. Eventually the county signed a memorandum of agreement to participate in the Secure Communities program, which in practice is very similar to the county's scaled-back resolution and makes it essentially redundant. Nonetheless, Prince William County spent $1.3 million on start-up costs and continues to spend $700,000 annually to maintain a police unit that specializes in "criminal aliens."[5] A report evaluating the outcomes of the ordinance commissioned by the county found that the policy had "seriously disrupted police-community relations in the County, at least temporarily."[6] It went on to note that the ordinance had had a significant negative impact on Hispanics' trust in county government, desire to live in the county, and perception of life in the county. Although relations and trust levels had improved again since the uproar over the resolution began, it was clear that it had driven a wedge between Hispanic immigrants and the rest of the community. Among its conclusions, the report stated that "the policy created fear and a sense of being unwelcome among immigrants in general."[7]

A Practical and Affordable Model

Jupiter has gone against the anti-immigrant tide that swept over Hazleton, Riverside, Prince William County, and many other localities around the country. Unlike these towns, Jupiter did not attempt to use local policy to make symbolic statements about national immigration policy. Jupiter is not a so-called sanctuary city, as anti-immigration groups (such as FAIR and FLIMEN) are apt to claim. The local police in Jupiter collaborate with immigration authorities when asked to do so, and there are no local ordinances prohibiting the Jupiter police from asking anyone about his or her immigration status. Jupiter has thus not had to spend millions of dollars defending itself against lawsuits for implementing unconstitutional anti-immigrant ordinances. Those who oppose El Sol claim that Jupiter spent $1.9 million buying a building for the Center, but in fact the town had plans to purchase the building prior to the creation of El Sol and still intends to eventually utilize the property for town expansion. As Councilman Robert Friedman pointed out in a letter to the editor of the *Palm Beach Post*, "[T]he property was purchased in order to provide room to expand the municipal complex, which it adjoins. The property was under contract in October of 2003 and the closing took place in November of 2005."[8]

The town is El Sol's landlord and thus pays for structural improvements and some maintenance to the building (such as the roof), but the cost is minimal compared to the cost of enforcing immigration-related ordinances and balanced against the value added by El Sol. Councilman Jim Kuretski sums up the town's perspective on El Sol, from a fiscal standpoint: "As an elected official, it is a no-brainer. We just enabled this to happen with the little work we did. This is the single most cost-effective expenditure the town has in the entire budget. I am a fiscal conservative, and there is no greater investment on the part of the town government than El Sol. When you think of the value that it brings back: it is like putting one buck in and getting one hundred back. One just has to look at where we were and where we are now." As Councilman Kuretski explains, not only is the cost of El Sol to the town of Jupiter minimal, but it is a worthy investment with high returns.

Each year El Sol provides a variety of services for all Jupiter residents with an annual budget of just over $200,000. Every quarter the El Sol center submits a report to the town, outlining its services and their estimated financial value to the community. In 2010 El Sol provided services totaling an estimated $883,044 to residents of Jupiter. This is an extremely conservative estimate, including only the costs of programs and volunteer hours and excluding the actual value added and costs saved by El Sol's programs to produce a healthier community, greater English literacy, better-trained workers, and more informed Jupiter residents. While those who oppose El Sol and the town of Jupiter's role in supporting the organization frequently accuse the town of using "taxpayer dollars" to fund El Sol, that is simply not the case. The annual budget for El Sol continues to come entirely from private donations and grants.

PRACTICAL APPROACHES TO MANAGING IMMIGRATION

Unauthorized immigration generates a series of complaints from across the political spectrum in the United States. The purported inability or unwillingness of new immigrants to learn English and the burden they represent for hospitals and emergency rooms are some of the oft-cited complaints levied against unauthorized immigrants. Another common complaint is that unauthorized immigrants take jobs for such low wages that American workers are unable to compete. The same problem, seen from a different perspective, is that unautho-rized immigrants become victims of employers who pay them meager wages knowing that they have little recourse against such violations. Despite the fact that academic studies consistently show that immigrants are more often vic-tims than perpetrators of crimes, the two continue to be associated in the minds of many.[9] Especially after the terrorist attacks of September 11, 2001, unautho-rized immigration has also been framed in terms of national security. The image of people living "in the shadows" resonates with Americans across the political spectrum. Interestingly, while those who oppose El Sol are quick to vocalize all these complaints, El Sol in fact addresses precisely these issues in very practical ways at the local level.

A general complaint about immigrants today is that they are not assimilat-ing properly and in particular not learning English fast enough. According to some critics, the system today accommodates immigrants' supposed unwill-ingness to learn. The protesters outside El Sol frequently held up signs high-lighting this point, demanding that immigrants "learn English" and decrying the need to "press 2 for English." Ironically, while they were demanding that El Sol shut down, they ignored the fact that every year hundreds of people are learn-ing English at El Sol. There are two different English programs at El Sol, and in 2010 almost three hundred students increased one level in their English profi-ciency through them. In a 2009 survey of El Sol users, 60 percent of the sample said that English classes were an important service, second only to the labor program (83 percent). In short, El Sol's clients are eager to learn English, and El Sol provides them with the opportunity do so. For students of immigrant assimilation this comes as no surprise, since studies of today's immigrants sug-gest that they are learning English at a rate faster than immigrants in previous generations did.[10] Despite alarmist claims to the contrary, the United States today continues to be a graveyard for non-English languages.

During the first Republican presidential debate of 2011 the question of unauthorized immigrants was framed in terms of whether or not the child of an "illegal immigrant" should receive care at an emergency room. Clearly, access to medical care and other social services remains one of the most salient immigration-related issues for the American electorate. It is also certainly true that in communities across the United States the majority of the unauthorized immigrant population is uninsured and lacks sufficient access to preventive care. In Jupiter, however, El Sol has a Health Committee, which addresses these needs by providing early screenings, preventive care, health referrals, and health education. Through community partners in 2010 alone, El Sol provided over thirteen thousand dollars' worth of pro bono medical services to Jupiter residents and helped 480 individuals with health-related issues, including vaccinations and HIV/AIDS testing and education. While El Sol is not in a position to provide health insurance to the client population it serves, it is on the front lines of preventive health services and thus reduces costs to local emergency rooms by preventing or avoiding unnecessary visits and referring clients to available health services.

Another popular charge against immigrants in new destination communities is that they drive down wages and make it impossible for the American worker to compete. The biggest protest in opposition to El Sol was the 2009 "Save the American Worker Rally," during which protesters argued that El Sol was undermining their ability to get jobs. Once again it is hard to dispute that in open-air day labor sites where work is often scarce and immigrants may accept extremely low wages in order to secure a day's work. A nationwide study found that wages at these sites are indeed very low; on average day laborers earn less than fifteen thousand dollars annually, putting them below the poverty line.[11] The same survey found that 49 percent of day laborers had been denied payment for work they had already completed and 48 percent had been underpaid. While El Sol does not directly negotiate wages with employers, the simple fact that they have to register at the center encourages higher wages (certainly above minimum wage) and prevents wage theft. Workers at El Sol also have access to legal assistance in case of wage disputes with employers. Furthermore, the fact that the hiring process is ordered and managed by El Sol discourages the race to the lowest possible wage among workers common at open-air hiring sites. Although the center does not formally "set" wages, the Workers' Council and volunteers suggest fair wage rates for employers and employees based on the number of hours to be worked and prevailing local wages. Thus, moving workers from the street to El Sol has likely increased local wage rates rather than driven down wages. Simply put, the job sector in which day laborers work is not in direct competition with those of most native-born workers in the Jupiter area. Asked to explain the fact that El Sol no longer faces major opposition in Jupiter, Father Don Finney explained, "I think there is not a whole lot of opposition because the jobs they fulfill aren't the type of jobs that people in Jupiter are clamoring after. They want the more professional type jobs. They are not competing with Guatemalans who work at the car wash or something."

A related concern with immigrant labor is the fact that unauthorized immigrants are often subject to abuses and mistreatment at work. The complaint in this case is not only that immigrants themselves are abused but also that this abuse lowers the overall standards for American workers. In other words, employers who do not wish to uphold the basic labor standards will become less likely to hire American workers because they will seek immigrant workers who may be less willing or able to file complaints. Immigrant workers, and especially day laborers, are indeed subject to several forms of abuse above and beyond wage theft. A study of day laborers found rampant abuse: 44 percent of day laborers had been denied food, water, and breaks by their employers; 32 percent had worked more hours than agreed to with the employer; 28 percent had been threatened or insulted by the employer; 27 percent had been abandoned at the work site by an employer; and 18 percent had been subject to violence by their employer.[12] The anonymity that the informal labor market provides employers facilitates these abuses. Once again this anonymity is eliminated by El Sol. Employers must register, and they are therefore more likely to uphold basic labor standards. The day labor market may continue to be relatively unregulated, but El Sol provides workers with access to resources through which they can report abuses, and in most cases this knowledge is sufficient to curb mistreatment on the part of employers. Although the legal office at El Sol fields many complaints from workers who have experienced wage theft and other abuses, none of those complaints were generated by people hired at the El Sol Neighborhood Resource Center (they come primarily from workers who find employment through other means such as personal referrals).

Despite clear evidence to the contrary, the American public continues to associate immigration and crime. The mere presence of unauthorized immigrants in the United States serves for many as evidence of a general disregard for American laws, and thus the cognitive leap from "illegal immigrant" to "criminal" becomes an easy one to make. The perception of high immigrant involvement in gangs, drugs, and other criminal activity is prevalent and often at the root of the fear that divides communities. But the fact is that unauthorized immigrants who are afraid of having contact with the police are often the victims of crimes and are unlikely to report those crimes. Day laborers are especially susceptible to crime because they are paid in cash and are unlikely to have bank accounts. El Sol's financial literacy programs help to address this issue, as workers are encouraged to open bank accounts and deposit their funds into those accounts.

More important, El Sol has become a trusted community institution where immigrants can feel safe talking to the police and other authorities to report crimes, thus making it more likely that criminals will be caught and removed from the Jupiter community. In combination with more aggressive code enforcement and community policing, the Jupiter police department has had significant success in removing criminal elements from the community. El Sol continues to play a key role in the relationship between the Police Department and the immigrant community in Jupiter, as throughout the year the police make several presentations on public safety at El Sol, ranging from practical issues such as bike safety to warnings about unscrupulous notaries or other criminals. According to the "Uniform Crime Report" of the Federal Bureau of Investigation (FBI), the number of violent crimes reported in Jupiter in 2010 had gone down over the past four years.[13]

Perhaps most important, El Sol does a great deal to, as President Obama is fond of saying, "bring people out of the shadows." The improved relationship between the Police Department and the immigrant community brokered by El Sol is a great benefit, but El Sol does much more to make Jupiter a safer place to live. As of March 2011 more than two thousand Jupiter residents were registered at the center. Each member has a picture ID with personal information, address, nationality, and other data on the card. El Sol ID cards are recognized by the local library and other public and private organizations in the area. Information about each member's job skills, positions worked, and employer feedback is also stored in the center's database. Although a significant portion of El Sol's clients are likely unauthorized, they are certainly no longer living in the shadows. El Sol has built a relationship of trust with the immigrant community and the town of Jupiter. Immigrants who live in Jupiter feel safe providing their personal information to El Sol. In turn El Sol maintains these data, making the community safer. The logical result is that it would be much more difficult for someone looking to "hide" in the shadows to do so in the town of Jupiter.

Because workers must register at El Sol to seek day labor, unauthorized criminal aliens would be deterred from seeking work in town. Furthermore, because the immigrants now have a more open and trusting relationship with local authorities, the immigrant community itself is more likely to report the presence of such individuals in its midst. Jill Hanson tells the story of one young worker who approached a staff member during El Sol's first year, which aptly illustrates this point.

> Early on, a worker came to her. A very sweet young guy, maybe he was seventeen or eighteen or so at the time. He told her that he had done a very bad thing and could not tell anybody about it. She talked to Lee, and she decided that he should tell me because I am a lawyer so I could keep it secret if it needed to be kept secret. We were wondering what the heck he could have done that was so bad that he couldn't tell her about it—they

were close. It turned out that he had been picked up on Center Street [before the center opened] and had been taken to work at a grow house [indoor hydroponic marijuana farm] in another county. He had been driven there and worked up there I think for two or three days in a series of grow houses. Then they flew him back here and threatened him. If he told anybody about it, he would be killed. The staff member acted as an interpreter, and he told me about it. I had a police officer friend at the time who was working on this whole grow house investigation, so I called him. He came and took a statement from him. Ultimately, bottom line, he now has a visa because he was able to help. He never had to testify at trial, but I guess they brought down a lot of bad guys because of his information. The guy that he had been working for was the kingpin of the whole group, and he came to Jupiter to pick somebody up from Center Street! I'm thinking surely before El Sol that he [the worker] wouldn't have had anybody to talk to, no recourse.

JUPITER IS NOT ALONE

Jupiter's El Sol represents an innovative and practical way to manage the effects of day labor and immigration in a local community. While more restrictive immigration policies have captured the limelight recently, there are well over one hundred organized day labor hiring sites such as El Sol in the United States.[14] As primarily symbolic statements aimed at federal lawmakers, restrictive policies such as Arizona's SB1070 and Hazleton's Illegal Immigration Relief Act Ordinance garner the lion's share of media attention. Integrative policies, however, are far more practical in quietly and competently managing the effects of immigration in the United States. Sixty-four cities, among them Philadelphia, San Francisco, Seattle, and Houston, have passed ordinances that in practice prevent the local police from sharing or collecting immigration-related information, except in felony cases.[15] Localities around the United States have gone even further. For example, New Haven, Connecticut, issues municipal identification cards to its residents, regardless of immigration status. These cards can be used within New Haven as a legally recognized form of identification to access services.[16] Furthermore, *matrículas consulares* issued by Mexican consulates in the United States are recognized as a proper form of identification by over 1,000 police agencies, nearly 400 cities, and more than 150 counties.[17]

While Jupiter is not a sanctuary city and does not issue its own identification cards, the town is not alone in pursuing positive, practical responses to manage the problems generated by antiquated and inadequate national immigration policies. Although each local community struggling with day labor and other immigration-related issues is different, many of the lessons from the Jupiter experience are applicable to other communities. It may be that the Jupiter experience can help other communities to turn the tide in favor of policies focused on immigrant integration.

THE PILLARS OF EL SOL

Reflecting on the first five years since El Sol opened, there are a number of key elements that have been critical to its success, some related to the process of lobbying for the center and others in terms of operating it. The coalition that emerged to support the creation of a center in Jupiter was held up primarily by four "pillars": a local group representing the immigrant community (Corn Maya Inc.), a local university (primarily through the Wilkes Honors College of FAU), the religious community (primarily through Saint Peter and eventually Catholic Charities), and sympathetic members of the town staff and elected officials. Each of these pillars provided critical support in the process of moving Jupiter's Town Council toward seriously considering a resource center. Prior to the opening of El Sol, the ethnic and religious homogeneity of Mayan immigrants in Jupiter created in-group solidarity and facilitated mobilization. As outlined in chapter 2, the initial group of Jacaltecos was able to use cultural and religious ties to mobilize a base of support by organizing the first fiesta on the university grounds. When the immigrant community first began organizing, it relied heavily on bonding social capital—ties to others like themselves.[18] This bonding social capital was important to generate solidarity and organize people around a common goal and a common identity. Jupiter's immigrants drew on the strength of their transnational connections as well to mobilize themselves and refound the nonprofit Corn Maya Inc., which would initiate the pilot resource center and articulate the needs of the immigrant community to the Town and other organizations. As Corn Maya's president, Patricio Silvestre, puts it, "There is a bridge between our communities. There is a bridge between our community in Jupiter and in Jacaltenango and another bridge between Corn Maya and the town. So people think of Corn Maya and El Sol as two sister organizations that help the migrant community."

As Silvestre notes, a second key factor in mobilizing for a center in Jupiter was that bonding social capital was translated into bridging social capital with local community groups. The immigrant community did not mobilize in isolation; it sought and found connections with nonimmigrant Jupiter residents.

The tight-knit immigrant community successfully formed links first with the local university and later with local churches and political groups. Educational and religious institutions became crucial bridges to the community, providing resources and garnering support from students, residents, and parishioners. Silvestre notes that the university connection was an important part of the lobbying process.

> When Corn Maya started up there was also help with some other organizations. They helped us with some statistics and information. The studies they carried out in Jupiter helped us because we had statistics now. Studies are good so you can present them to an organization like the town. The type of information they gave us is hard for us to gather. The information that they gave us helped us with the numbers and exact things; we cannot present projects with ambiguous numbers and data. They helped us present our case to the town, so that they could have a different understanding of the migrants here in Jupiter.

While data from the Ford Foundation study were important to the process, student interns from the university also played a critical role. The initial needs assessment done in the immigrant community could not have been completed without student interns. When the Corn Maya office reopened in Jupiter it was primarily staffed by interns. Today El Sol's director continues to credit them for their role in making El Sol run. A former intern herself, Jocelyn Skolnik explains:

> I have to give them so much credit. We have had about fifteen interns, most of them from the Honors College of FAU. They have been the most committed, responsible, mature, thoughtful, dedicated, and sincere; they are seriously amazing. I'm a little bit tough, so every single one of our interns has exceeded the expectations from their schools. They exceed their hours, participate in many more activities than initially discussed. They really believe in our mission. They have encouraged others to become interns. The interns have played a critical role in helping us build capacity. They have been the ones who support us with quarterly reports, prepare proposals, improve our ESL curriculum, etc.

Councilman Jim Kuretski also emphasized this point when asked about the key factors that made El Sol possible: "Each volunteer, or many of them at least, brought different entities in. For example, we would have never had the energy of the students without the connection to FAU. Before we even got involved in any organized manner, you had students involved. Then, when El Sol opened up, we still had that steady base for nighttime English classes of the student volunteers from FAU. What would have happened if we didn't have that? They are still here to this day."

The university also provided faculty with technical and language skills who served as liaisons with the immigrant community. In the case of Jupiter, the Ford Foundation grant also brought researchers from Guatemala who worked with FAU professors conducting local research and helped to build trust in the immigrant community. On the side of town authorities, having local academics viewed as experts on the immigrant groups involved also provides greater avenues for communication and collaboration. As Town Manager Andy Lukasik explains:

> We had the right individuals and institutions: Sister Marta, Mike, Jill, the university, each bringing resources and people. The volunteers . . . your institutional positions brought the volunteers along. All these people came with you who represented the community, and they were willing to do all this work. It [El Sol] is not a government-run program. It is a community-run program. That was key. If the community was not committed, it wouldn't have worked. We wouldn't have forced it down everybody's throats. Ultimately it would have failed. . . . The role of Saint Peter was also critical. That church won Jim Kuretski over.

Jim Kuretski notes the key role that trust played in the formation of support for the center: "That is why trust is so important. By the time that we did act and by the time we opened up the Center I saw two distinct groups. One was Corn Maya, and the other one was Sister Marta through the religious initiative. Both groups were building trust, and that trust was so important to accomplish change."

Lukasik's and Kuretski's point about the role of religious institutions in the process of opening and running El Sol cannot be underestimated. Religious organizations are some of the only social organizations open to new migrant groups. Churches provided the spaces, resources, lay leaders, and clergy who helped to mobilize both the immigrants and those who share the pews with them. Without question, Saint Peter took the lead in this respect, hosting the original coalition meetings with PEACE and representatives of Catholic Charities, bringing in Sister Marta, who would become a fixture at El Sol, and providing scores of volunteers to staff the kitchen and other El Sol programs. Father Finney of Saint Peter explains: "It is almost like a case study in strategic alliances. If the church tried to do this alone, it wouldn't work. If Corn Maya tried to do this alone, it wouldn't work. If the town tried to do it alone, it wouldn't work. It had to have all the players there, each bringing their piece of the puzzle."

The fourth pillar supporting efforts to open the center was town staff. Early in the process, the town manager's office opened discussions and began the work of bringing stakeholders to the table. Representatives of the town of Jupiter went through a long process of education about the immigrant community and how other cities had dealt with the issue of day labor. After doing their homework, they worked tirelessly to craft a comprehensive solution that combined enforcement (in terms of housing codes and other neighborhood issues) and the opening of a center. It was particularly important to create nonconfrontational opportunities for interaction between the Town Council members and representatives of the immigrant community such as the sister city event. As Sister Marta points out, "The town really seemed to be working *with* us; they were not that negative. That is how I felt, too, [that] we didn't have to confront them. There was no need; we were in a dialogue and they were also part of the dialogue." The day laborers and contractors also had to be educated about the benefits of using El Sol and leaving Center Street. This required a nearly year-long process of meetings and trust building between leaders of the immigrant community, the town, and local businesses. Again, Sister Marta explains:

> That is what I consider my part there: trying to help build trust. It wasn't easy. We tried to communicate with them. We were trying to tell them, "If we open a center, it is for your own safety." "Well, is immigration going to come?" "I cannot promise anything. I just can tell you that you're going to be safer there. Immigration can come here to the streets too. At least you will have a space." I think all of that helped. We had preopenings. That is very important. We tried to create the trust in them and to really open up. So this was all before the center opened. . . . That is why it was so "easy" for us when we opened because they knew what it was. Communication, I really believe in communication. I think people need to know what is going on and be part of it. If there are just things there for people, they might not respond, but if they are doing it themselves they get involved.

A number of other specific factors also contributed to the successful effort to open El Sol. Without question, the fact that Catholic Charities was able to procure funding for the first year tipped the balance for members of the council who were on the fence about the center. As Corn Maya discovered while running the pilot program, a center simply cannot be successful unless it has the resources to hire staff and the facilities to house the workers. Since resource centers must be open long hours and generally seven days a week to keep workers from returning to the streets, the costs for staff are likely to be substantial. As Mike Richmond points out, procuring sufficient funding to open El Sol in the first year was a critical turning point in the process: "I think one of the turning points was when Catholic Charities stepped up. I don't say that because I happen to be a member of that faith, but I say that because we had no money and no one else was stepping forward. The town was taking some heat about wanting to do something and spending taxpayer money. The turning point, I think, came when this agency stepped up and said that they would help."

It is also undeniable that the process of procuring the building and its physical location were crucial in the evolution of El Sol. As a property that was already under contract for the town, the church building provided both an ideal facility and a politically more feasible option for the council. Although not every community has such a building available, Andy Lukasik explains the importance of the structure and its proximity to other town services.

Some of the centers were cast out and left on their own in industrial areas that were not very nice. We had the benefit of the structure itself. The town acquired it not knowing that it was going to be used for this purpose. We owned it, it was there, and it wasn't being used. We still wouldn't be using it. You might as well have it be used to address this pretty significant issue that we had in our community. It was another resource. We are the envy of anybody else who ever operated a center: look at the space that we have, the resources that we have there, the proximity to the government, the way that the government has supported it. We don't run it, and we wanted it that way. We wanted it to be arm's length to some degree because it was always supposed to be a community-led program. Even with that, we have involvement; we still play a supporting role when needed.

Lee McCarthy also pointed to the critical role of the actual facility in making El Sol a success. In McCarthy's opinion:

The building is ideal for our situation. . . . The physical building has had such a big impact. One of the reasons it came about so easily is that there

The main entrance to the El Sol building, 2012 (Courtesy of Sandra Lazo de la Vega)

was such a good place for everybody to come and room to do everything that needed to be done. I see only good things happening as long as there is a good physical location; otherwise you can't do it. The fact that the building is on the campus of the town: I always made a point to tell people when they called to ask about the location, I always said, "Next to the police station." It preempts a lot of questions. I can't even envision what would happen without the building.

BEST PRACTICES FOR SUCCESS

Once open, El Sol brought together a series of "best practices" drawn from many of the other centers around the country. The coalition of center supporters chose a centrally located building owned by the town, engaged both employers and laborers in the process of developing the hiring process, and passed a no-solicitation ordinance concurrently with the opening of the center. Other key elements of the best practices that make up the El Sol model include the formation of the Workers' Council to provide input on an organized and fair hiring process and establishing a committed group of volunteers by providing them with meaningful and fulfilling roles in the daily operations of the center. As Kuretski points out, by borrowing the proven strategies of other centers, Jupiter was able to construct a model that exceeded its own early expectations: "We have had visits from representatives from other centers, from centers that we had looked up to, centers we had researched and thought, "Hopefully, one day we will be like them." When we got visits from them, they were impressed . . . [and] we were hearing we had one-upped them. It really felt good. It re-affirmed what we did set out to do: we set out to be the best of the best by not reinventing the wheel but by replicating the best attributes of other centers."

Center director Jocelyn Skolnik explains the need for flexibility and transparency in all aspects of operations at the Center.

> At the beginning the guys didn't think the system was fair, so you have to be very transparent. I think you have to be open and trusting and most of all, organized. Have your plan in place, study other places hard. We did; we sent people to see how other places worked. Don't spend time reinventing the wheel; tweak the wheel. You have to involve the workers and make them active participants. You have to listen and be consciously involving them. If you are inflexible you will be in for surprises all the time. Things will evolve, and you have to adapt; that is critical.

For El Sol, part of that adaptability and input comes through the Workers' Council. As Skolnik puts it, "The Workers' Council has exposed its members to the inner workings of a dynamic organization, its volunteer spirit, and committee structure, and has provided the groundwork for its members to become more engaged and active members of the community." She tells the story of one worker who embodies this process.

> Francisco was one of the founding members of El Sol's Workers' Council. He is originally from Guatemala and registered with El Sol in 2007. He was among the first workers to get very involved in the formation of our center rules. Francisco served for two years on the Workers' Council and provided great leadership to the workers. He would come in to El Sol to look for day jobs but would also encourage workers to collaborate and volunteer around the center. He found permanent employment, and still dedicated his Saturday mornings to El Sol. After a full week's worth of work he would come in early morning on Saturday to volunteer in the kitchen. He also worked with El Sol to develop a basic literacy program

for workers helping those who do not know how to read and write in Spanish. Francisco is one of El Sol's success stories. He has been promoted to foreman at his job and leads a crew of workers. On top of that, he also is an exemplary student. As an intern at Corn Maya, in 2006, I taught him level 1 ESL classes. Recently, when I started teaching ESL at Jupiter High School, I was pleasantly surprised to find him in my level 5 and 6 English class, the most advanced class offered in Jupiter High School's adult education program.

From the beginning the center was conceived of as a place where the workers would have a voice in constructing policies. Not just the elected council but the entire assembly of workers would have the opportunity to vote. As former El Sol president Jill Hanson explains:

I put it [the Workers' Council] into the original bylaws of El Sol. The Workers' Council had voted on the rules and had voted to accept them. I thought that was fine. He [a representative of the National Day Labor Organizing Network (NDLON)] said that we had to have a vote of the whole assembly. He said the assembly was the foundation, the basis for the power of the workers. I was scared. They voted for it. They all voted for the rules. Now I see how important it was because it gives the rules legitimacy. I guess this comes from NDLON but also from my background in the trade union movement. . . . If the workers do not participate in it and do not buy into it, then it will not work.

But it is not just the workers who have come to adopt El Sol as "their place." The volunteers, many of whom come to the center on a daily basis, also feel a sense of belonging at El Sol. Andi Cleveland, one of El Sol's key volunteers, explains how she first came to feel "at home" as a volunteer at El Sol.

How I found El Sol was literally driving by day in and day out as I was looking for a house. I saw men going in and out in groups and the American flag and I wondered what was happening there. I had never actually experienced something like that before, never seen anything like that. So I just stopped one day and I came in the door. Sister Marta and Eileen were standing there. Sister Marta turned around and said to me, "Well, what took you so long?" I don't know if she thought I was somebody else or what! I don't know why she said that to me, but there I was!

I guess I was struck by the warmth that I felt right away. Obviously there was a great need. When I came here, I knew nobody. I had lived in the same place for twenty years. Things there were very familiar and safe. I felt like I was at home with family when I came. There wasn't any judging. . . . That's one thing I like about El Sol; nobody judges you. You can be rich, poor, old, young . . . and you are here to work, for a job, and that's it. It really satisfied what I was looking for in a volunteer organization.

Cleveland is not alone in her sense of satisfaction volunteering at El Sol. Almost universally the volunteers at El Sol express the immediacy of their experience there. Lee McCarthy saw this satisfaction firsthand in the many volunteers she recruited and organized for the center.

The men are so appreciative. The volunteers stay because it's not like licking stamps. You make a meal, you serve someone, and they are full. It is hands-on, instant gratification. You get to see what is going on. You really feel like you are making a difference. Sometimes with other nonprofits you're such a small cog in such a big wheel; you may feel like

Sally Isham, volunteer coordinator at El Sol, 2012. The paintings in the background are by workers at El Sol. (Courtesy of Sandra Lazo de la Vega)

you are doing busywork. With this there is no middle person: you are there, the person you are helping is there, and it's done. They're so great, so appreciative. We are all selfish—truly I believe that people do things to feel good. I think the fact that the people here who are being served are so grateful, the synergy is just there. It's easy to get and keep volunteers when there is this level of gratification. The secret ingredient is probably that you have so many people willing to give up so much of their time for no salary.

As Jill Hanson points out, the volunteers are important not only on a day-to-day basis inside El Sol but also because they represent El Sol to the community at large.

[Another] key ingredient is the volunteer base. They are key from the point of view of the work that they contribute, but also politically they are really key. From the election before that, our volunteers knew that the election was important. These are all people who are active in the community; they are committed to El Sol, committed to the town of Jupiter. A lot of us became active in the campaigns [for Town Council], and I think it helped to get these people reelected. Also in terms of just carrying the message back to the rest of the community. The message is that this is a good thing, it has helped the whole community, it is nothing to be afraid of. People carry back the things we do here. That has been really important.

REFRAMING IMMIGRATION

Boiled down to its essence, El Sol's success in Jupiter is about the practical management of real problems and the human interactions that take place on a day-to-day basis between immigrants and the native born to address those problems. Board members, volunteers, and staff at El Sol do not speak with one voice on immigration policy, but they do share an understanding of the human dimensions of the issue and an appreciation for the complexities of immigration and the immigration debate. Andi Cleveland explains: "The problems that we are dealing with here are human problems, not policy or immigration problems. I think that is what is at the core of this place. I think the public recognizes that and they are willing to help for that cause. It's a win-win situation for the town of Jupiter, the people, and the volunteers here. I don't think volunteers come in and think of immigration politics. I think they see more of the humanity here."

Cleveland's point about "seeing the humanity" may not foster a single unified position on national immigration policy, but it does begin to puncture the negative myths and abstractions that reinforce the gridlock in the national immigration debate. El Sol's volunteers, staff, and community supporters come face to face with the daunting hurdles faced by unauthorized immigrants in their daily lives. Many of the day-to-day problems addressed at El Sol stem from the immigration status of the center's clients. One day it is a mother who arrives at the center in tears because she has been stopped for driving without a license while taking her children to school and fears picking them up because she will have to pass the same officer stationed outside the school. The next day it is young man asking for help translating court documents related to his immigration case. As Jill Hanson, who provides legal counsel for many El Sol clients, explains, Palm Beach County's courts are filled with immigrants facing similar problems: "So . . . on average probably once a week I take a person to court. It is almost always driving without a license. . . . Occasionally there are other things, but it is almost always driving without a license. I remember one time Juanita got a ticket for driving without a license. She looked around and asked me, 'Do they have one court for immigrants and another one for everybody else?' In all innocence she asked me that, but if you go and just look, that is what it looks like. It still is very bad."

El Sol cannot issue Florida driver's licenses or change state or federal immigration laws, but it can and does assist immigrants as they negotiate the many barriers to integration in a new destination such as Jupiter. The Family Literacy program helps mothers to negotiate the complicated bureaucracy of the Palm Beach County school system. Access to limited public services (such as the public library) and the banking system for new immigrants opens new pathways for literary and financial education. Civics training and code compliance education not only help new immigrants to avoid code violations but also help them to become more engaged residents of Jupiter. Opportunities for service in community cleanups and property restoration through El Sol provide an increased sense of ownership and belonging in the community. Through El Sol, the town's new immigrants are beginning to feel that they belong in Jupiter and Jupiter belongs to them. Moving forward, this provides an opportunity for Jupiter to evolve as a single and more unified community, rather than a community divided by fear and mistrust. No matter what happens in terms of immigration reform at the national level, Jupiter will be in a better position to positively integrate its immigrant community than localities that have chosen to go the punitive route.

Moreover, the enforcement-only approach of Hazleton and similar communities does nothing to move the immigration debate in any direction. The costly and symbolic ordinances adopted in Hazleton and elsewhere may deflect immigrants to other areas, but they are unlikely to cause them to leave the country. Given what we know about the sacrifices immigrants such as Ulises have made to get here, and given the fact that many unauthorized families are rooted in the United States via children or family members who are citizens, they are primarily here to stay. Not only will they stay; they will also carry a distinct sense of alienation and rejection. The process of integration for these immigrants will be slow and difficult. If we conceive of the United States as an efficient immigrant integration machine, these punitive local enforcement initiatives are rapidly draining the oil that lubricates the moving parts. As a country we will be left to deal with the consequences in the form of a persistent and potentially oppositional and racially defined underclass.

Jupiter's experience with El Sol shows the plausibility of practical local solutions that address real problems effectively, reduce fear and alienation in communities, and have the potential to move the national immigration debate forward in a productive way. First, El Sol is a logical answer to the many real tensions that arise in communities undergoing rapid sociodemographic and economic change. El Sol has improved the quality of life in the neighborhoods where tensions began: today hundreds of day laborers no longer line Center Street, and complaints about public nuisances, littering, overcrowding, and code violations have all decreased. Even from the perspective of town authorities, El Sol has exceeded expectations in terms of addressing the practical quality-of-life issues it was initially proposed to address. Although the town has a no-solicitation ordinance on the books, the transition to El Sol has been so effective that to this day the ordinance has never been actively enforced. Father Finney neatly captures the sense of many Jupiter residents about El Sol's effectiveness in this respect: "It cleaned up the look on Center Street. They put [up] the nice lampposts and everything so that when you drive through it looks better. I think everyone in Jupiter takes a certain pride. . . . This is a pretty place. It is a nice place to live, and it has that nice quality. The schools are good. This is a nice place. Maybe even if you weren't sold on El Sol at the beginning, you will still like that it has solved the neighborhood problem of people standing around making it look bad."

Second, El Sol brings immigrants and the native born together in a way that reduces precisely the set of generalized fears that stymie productive discussions about immigration. As Jupiter residents come to better understand the forces propelling immigration, the challenges faced by immigrants, and the contributions they make to the community, many of those fears dissipate as the human face of immigration begins to emerge. When asked what advice she might offer to people in other towns going through the same process, Pine Gardens South resident Mary Anne Oblaczynski suggested:

> Look at the human part of the person. Don't look at the color of their skin, or the difference in the language, but look at why they are here. Try to look at the other side. Try to look outside of their difference. Are they that much different? Try to understand, talk to the people. Still to this day, the biggest thing is to realize that the influx of people coming in to your neighborhood . . . they are not there to tear it down. They are there because it is someplace they want to live because it's nice. Look at the human side of the person. Stop looking at numbers, stop looking at politics, stop looking at class. If you were in their shoes, would you do something different?

Finally, the process of reducing fears and bridging differences takes place in two directions, as immigrants also begin to feel more welcome as they make personal connections with volunteers, employers, and neighbors in an environment that was previously closed and even hostile. As Mayor Karen Golonka explains, the process goes beyond El Sol to include local government: "As mayor it is important in those situations to make sure that they feel that the town *is* welcoming. I am representing how the town feels. It is important that the immigrant population feels that, particularly to counterbalance the hostility. It is important that they feel that they are welcome. Of course they get that at El Sol, but here the new immigrants are looking at government in this different context. If I can put a friendly face on government then that is important. Maybe that will affect their next interaction with an authority figure or government."

While it will certainly take many years for the immigrant community in Jupiter to feel fully integrated, we can safely say that the process has begun. El Sol's greatest strength is that the lives (and roles) of the volunteers and clients are increasingly connected. An event that transpired at the Center on Christmas Eve, 2010, provides a telling example. A worker entered and approached the director as the center was about to close. When she asked how she could help him, he looked down and reached out his hand with forty dollars and said, "When I lost my job I came to the center and I was able to improve my English and find steady work. . . . I know it is not much, but I wanted to give something back to El Sol." There could hardly be a better measurable outcome of positive integration than this young man's gesture.

ACKNOWLEDGMENTS

El Sol takes its name from dual sources. First, in Spanish *el sol* means "the sun." The founders of the organization believed that would be a fitting name for an organization in South Florida that seeks to bring people out of the shadows. Second, the center is named for Sol Silverman, the husband of the center's second president and key organizer, Jill Hanson. Sol Silverman was a lifelong activist who became an avid supporter of the center toward the end of his life. He was a frequent visitor to Town Council meetings and routinely wrote letters to the editor of the *Jupiter Courier*. Sol died in 2005 at the age of eighty-eight as the political battles surrounding the opening of the center were at their height. At one of his last Town Council meetings, he gave an impassioned speech on behalf of immigrant workers and implored the council to provide a location for the center. We cannot thank Sol and Jill enough for all they have done for the town of Jupiter, its immigrant community, and the institution of El Sol.

We are also extremely grateful to the many individuals and families who gave us their time not only to be interviewed but also to review our manuscript for accuracy. Special thanks to Jerónimo Camposeco, Juan Patricio Silvestre, Marcos Cota Diaz, Auricio Camposeco, Antonio Gelacio Delgado, Mario Gervacio and Antonio Quiñones, Juan Danilo Camposeco of Corn Maya Inc., and all the past and present members of the Workers' Council. Without their hard work El Sol would never have become a reality.

At the town of Jupiter, Andy Lukasik, Jim Kuretski, and Karen Golonka gave generously of their time not only for interviews but also in the process that led up to the opening of El Sol. Special thanks are due to Anne Lyons for her tireless work in community outreach for the town and to Madeleine Pavola for putting together the reams of background information necessary to piece together this story. Robert Lecky and Melinda Miller also played an unheralded but critical role as town employees in the years leading up to and after the founding of El Sol.

The board members, volunteers, and staff of El Sol also deserve special mention. Board members Mike Richmond, Lee McCarthy, Mary Anne Oblaczynski, and Sister Marta Lucía Tobón Gómez feature prominently in the manuscript and in the founding of El Sol. Center director Jocelyn Skolnik and volunteer kitchen coordinator Andi Cleveland were also interviewed at length for the book. We thank them deeply for what they do at El Sol but also for taking the time to share their stories with us.

On a day-to-day basis, the employees and volunteers at El Sol are the ones who make the place run. We would like to express our gratitude to Dora Valdivia, associate director of El Sol; Wilberto Luna, labor coordinator; and Betzy Rega, health coordinator. Board members Suzanne Cordero, Roger Buckwalter, Yvonne Santiago, Sheila Hirsch, Aileen Josephs, Frank Walsh, and Terry McFarland have also gone above and beyond in their work to make El Sol a success. Many of El Sol's board members are also frequent volunteers at the organization. We reserve special thanks for the leadership and generosity of our current president, Ed Ricci, and his wife, Mary Lupo. Without their support, El Sol might never have gotten over the initial hurdles of fund-raising and the transition from Catholic Charities to Corn Maya and the Friends of El Sol.

The volunteers are at the heart of El Sol, and the organization absolutely could not function without them. Fortunately for the organization, they are far too many to list here. But we would like to give special mention to Sally Isham, our volunteer coordinator, and Tom Choate, our information technology guru, as they appear in the pages of this book. Any attempt to recognize *all* the other individuals who devote time and effort to El Sol is doomed to fall short. We therefore offer this collective thanks to El Sol's greatest asset—its committed core of community volunteers.

At Catholic Charities, we would like to directly thank John Levin and Marisol Zequeira Burke for their support and enthusiasm, believing that El Sol could become a reality. It is clear that El Sol would never have gotten off the ground without Catholic Charities stepping in during the first year of operation. The representatives of People Engaged in Community Efforts (PEACE), Rosa María Montenegro, Rev. Donald Duncombe, and Aleem Fakir, also deserve special recognition, as their enthusiasm pushed the agenda of a resource center forward in Jupiter. At Saint Peter, Father Don Finney, Sherry Krasulsa, and Nora Ugalde were instrumental in forming links with members of the immigrant community and their hometowns in Guatemala.

The Wilkes Honors College of Florida Atlantic University also deserves recognition. As an interdisciplinary liberal arts and sciences college within the larger university, the Honors College has always supported local community engagement among its faculty and students. The student members of the Corn Maya Club and the many interns who have served at Corn Maya and El Sol over the years provided the enthusiasm and support to keep the process rolling for five years prior to the opening of El Sol. They continue to be key players in the English as a second language program and other El Sol outreach activities.

The Latin American and Caribbean Center (LACC) at Florida International University also deserves special acknowledgment and gratitude. Sandra is especially in debt to Dr. Ana Maria Bidegain and Dr. Sherry Johnson for providing her with constructive feedback and constant encouragement throughout the process of writing this book.

Without support from the Ford Foundation, the research that informs this book could not have been conducted. Special thanks are due to Sheila Davaney for her belief in the project, Philip Williams and Manuel Vásquez of the University of Florida for directing it, and Carol Girón Solórzano and Silvia Irene Palma of the Central American Institute for Social Studies and Development (INCEDES) and the Guatemalan team for their outstanding research in communities of destination such as Jupiter, as well as in communities of origin in Guatemala.

We also owe a debt of gratitude to the staff and fellows at the Woodrow Wilson International Center for Scholars. The center provided the perfect balance of encouragement and direction necessary for work on this project to proceed during the summer of 2011. We are especially thankful to Johanna Sharp, John and Judy Steigenga, and Carolyn VanMeter, who provided valuable input on early drafts of the book.

Tim would also like to thank Frank Huyler, who read and commented on various versions of the manuscript and provided critical advice along the way. Special thanks as well to Ted Murphy, who shared his extensive knowledge of Washington, D.C., and extended his hospitality during the summer of 2011. Sandra is especially thankful to Conchita Bayona, Claudia Lazo de la Vega, and Tyler Sloss for their love and support throughout her various academic endeavors and for putting up with her extended absences during work on the book.

We reserve special thanks for Gwen Walker of the University of Wisconsin Press, who believed in this project from the initial stages, and the outstanding external readers she recruited to provide feedback to us throughout the process. This book is dedicated to one of the newest additions to the town of Jupiter, Talia Skolnik, born on April 24, 2012, and to the memory of Town Council member Robert M. Friedman, who left us all too soon, on July 11, 2012.

NOTES

Introduction

1. The terms *illegal alien, undocumented immigrant*, and *unauthorized immigrant* are widely used in the popular media to refer to immigrants who are technically "out of status." In other words, the terms refer to individuals who either crossed the border without registering at a designated port of entry or have overstayed or otherwise violated the terms of their visas. However, each of the terms comes with significant baggage. Few illegal immigrants are actually undocumented—as many carry formal documents from their countries of origin. At the same time, labeling a group of individuals as "illegal" persons is both technically inaccurate (as these individuals are still persons covered under the equal protection clause of the Fourteenth Amendment) and dehumanizing (as we do not apply the term to individuals who commit other specific crimes—including rape and murder). Although all three terms are used at times within the text of this book, we favor the term *unauthorized* as it is more accurate (in terms of the specific law violated) and less pejorative. We utilize the term "illegal" only when directly quoting or paraphrasing our sources.

2. El Sol, Jupiter's Neighborhood Resource Center, "2011 Annual Report," http://friendsofelsol.org/wp-content/uploads/2011/12/Q-IV-FINAL-2011.pdf (accessed July 6, 2012). "According to the Florida Governor's Commission on Volunteerism and Community Service, the value of volunteer contributions is estimated at $19.52 per hour. This is the amount [El Sol] assigns to calculate the value of [its] programs" (2).

3. Michael Rubinkam, "Pa. Town to Crack Down on Illegal Immigrants," *Pittsburgh Post Gazette*, June 20, 2006.

4. Monica W. Varsanyi, "Immigration Policing through the Backdoor: City Ordinances, the 'Right to the City,' and the Exclusion of Undocumented Day Laborers," *Urban Geography* 29, no. 1 (2008): 37.

5. Karla McKanders, "Welcome to Hazleton ('Illegal' Immigrants Beware): Local Employment Immigration Ordinances and What the Federal Government Must Do about It," *Loyola University Chicago Law Journal* 39, no. 1 (2007): 3–49, 9.

6. Margaret Hobbins, "The Day Laborer Debate: Small Town, U.S.A. Takes on Federal Immigration Law Regarding Undocumented Workers," *Modern American* 2, no. 3 (2006): 10–17, 10.

7. Bill Turque, "Herndon to Shut Down Center for Day Laborers," *Washington Post*, September 6, 2007. The Town Council had initially attempted to keep the center open but restricted access to those who could provide proof of residency or citizenship.

8. Florida Immigration Enforcement Act, 2010, bill proposed in the Florida Legislature, available at http://myfloridalegal.com/webfiles.nsf/WF/MRAY-888HAK/$file/ImmigrationBillDraft.pdf (accessed July 6, 2012), section 5, lines 210–14.

9. As the country's leading organization seeking to reduce immigration to the United States, FAIR is at the forefront of the anti-immigrant campaign. In 2007 the Southern Poverty Law Center classified FAIR as a hate group, citing several associations between it and white supremacist groups.

10. Programs such as 287(g) and Secure Communities are federal government initiatives that authorize local police forces to make immigration-related inquiries and arrests. These programs are purported to target "high-priority" populations (unauthorized immigrants who have committed felonies), but in reality the majority of those deported as a result of these programs are unauthorized immigrants who have not committed serious crimes.

11. Corn Maya Inc. is a 501(c)(3) nonprofit organization whose mission is to collaborate with local authorities, other nonprofit organizations, and educational institutions in order to promote cultural awareness, provide access to vital services, and initiate positive relationships between immigrant-sending and immigrant-receiving communities through educational and sustainable development initiatives. Corn Maya continues to operate an office in the El Sol center.

Chapter 1. From Back Burner to Center Stage

1. Brian Bandell, "WCI Sets Pace for Northern Palm Beach Development," *South Florida Business Journal*, August 23, 2004.

2. The town of Jupiter has a town manager and town council institutional form of government, which places day-to-day operations under the auspices of the town manager. This form of mayor-council system is sometimes referred to as a "weak mayor" system because the mayor has limited executive powers (budget making, appointments, etc.).

3. In 2002 Lukasik held the position of assistant town manager.

4. John Lantigua, "Suburbanites, Day Laborers at Odds in Jupiter," *Palm Beach Post*, February 16, 2004.

5. John Lantigua, "Guatemalan Official Empty-Handed in Jupiter Visit," *Palm Beach Post*, April 21, 2004.

6. Jennifer Brannock, "Initial Jupiter Labor Center Costs Could Be $1 Million," *Jupiter Courier*, June 6, 2004.

7. Linea Brown, "Group to Sue to Stop Labor Center," *Jupiter-Tequesta Hometown News*, September 2, 2005.

8. Federation for American Immigration Reform, "Confronting Illegal Day-Labor Issues in Your Community," adapted from Michael Hethmon, *The Immigration Reformer's Guide to Legal Success* (Washington, D.C.: FAIR Horizon Press, 2002).

9. Although it is based in Pompano Beach, FLIMEN and David Caulkett continued to be a presence in Jupiter until 2010 (years after the opening of the resource center and

the dissolution of JNAIL in 2006). Caulkett prompted a major incident at El Sol in 2008 when he initiated a confrontation while filming an employer leaving the building and threatened to turn the tape over to authorities.

CHAPTER 2. THE IMMIGRANT COMMUNITY IN JUPITER

1. The quotes from Jerónimo Camposeco in this chapter come from an extended written interview that was edited for grammar and syntax.

2. In Guatemala, the term *ladino* commonly refers to indigenous and nonindigenous people who have adopted nonindigenous forms of cultural expression.

3. Victor Montejo, *Voices from Exile* (Norman: University of Oklahoma Press, 1999), 52.

4. Douglas Massey, "Why Does Immigration Occur? A Theoretical Synthesis," in *The Handbook of International Migration*, ed. Charles Hirschman, Phillip Kasinitz, and Josh DeWind (New York: Russell Sage Foundation, 1999), 35–36.

5. Ibid., 43–47.

6. Ulises told us that he chose his pseudonym not only because it was the name on his false Mexican identification but also because *Ulysses* is his favorite book.

7. Ibid., 36–37.

8. Ibid., 40–43.

9. Michael Piore, *Birds of Passage: Migrant Labor and Industrial Societies* (Cambridge: Cambridge University Press, 1979), 35–43; Massey, "Why Does Immigration Occur?," 40.

10. Douglas Massey and Jorge Durand, eds., *Crossing the Border: Research from the Mexican Migration Project* (New York: Russell Sage Foundation, 2004).

11. Peggy Levitt, *The Transnational Villagers* (Berkeley: University of California Press, 2001).

12. The abbreviation ABC stands for the American Baptist Churches. The American Baptist Churches sued the INS on behalf of some Central American people whose asylum claims were being dismissed because the United States supported the governments that perpetrated the abuses they were fleeing. In other words, the INS was denying claims not because they lacked merit but rather for purely political reasons. The ABC and INS settled, and as part of the settlement the INS agreed to revisit claims that had been previously denied.

The abbreviation TPS stands for Temporary Protective Status, a special immigration status granted to some people who cannot safely return to their countries of origin due to a disaster (such as a hurricane or an earthquake).

Both TPS and ABC were having important impacts on the Guatemalan community during 1993–94, the time period to which Patricio is referring.

13. As a board member of Corn Maya Inc., FAU professor Timothy Steigenga served as the primary grant writer for the organization.

CHAPTER 3. DEBATING A COMMUNITY RESOURCE CENTER

1. Roger Buckwalter, "2004 Leaves Plenty of Positives," *Jupiter Courier*, December 2004.

2. Pamela Perez, "Foes of Day Laborer Center in Jupiter Protest," *Palm Beach Post*, January 30, 2005.

3. "Jupiter Does What's Right," editorial, *Sun Sentinel*, April 13, 2005.

4. "Jupiter Sets an Example on the Day-Labor Issue," editorial, *Palm Beach Post*, April 14, 2005.

5. Roger Buckwalter, "The Best of Intentions: Labor Backers Get Their Chance," *Jupiter Courier*, April 20, 2005.

6. Linea Brown, "One Step Closer: Site Chosen for Jupiter Labor Center," *Jupiter-Tequesta Hometown News*, April 15, 2005.

7. In 2004 Hethmon was the director of FAIR's legal arm, the Immigration Reform and Law Institute. According to his website, he helped write Arizona's infamous Support Our Law Enforcement and Safe Neighborhoods Act, which, among other provisions, directed police to stop and question individuals who were suspected to be undocumented. http://mikehethmon.com/home (accessed July 6, 2012).

8. Stephen Deere, "Resource Center Conflict Intensifies," *Sun Sentinel*, August 21, 2005.

9. Kit Bradshaw, "Groups Planning Lawsuit against Jupiter Labor Center," *Sun Sentinel*, August 14, 2005.

10. Linea Brown, "Group to Sue over Labor Center," *Jupiter-Tequesta Hometown News*, September 2, 2005.

11. Ibid.

12. Pamela Perez, "Jupiter Forges Ties with Guatemalans' Hometown," *Palm Beach Post*, August 7, 2005.

13. "Blessed and Welcome," editorial, *Palm Beach Post*, June 6, 2006.

14. "High Hopes for El Sol Success," editorial, *Jupiter Courier*, June 11, 2006.

CHAPTER 4. EL SOL IN THE SUNSHINE STATE

1. "Graduates Recognized for ESL, Computer Training," *El Sol Shines*, January 2011.

2. The workers' assembly is composed of all the workers registered at El Sol.

3. "El Sol Workers Pitch In and Paint," *El Sol Shines*, August 2010.

4. "Jupiter Does What's Right," editorial, *Sun Sentinel*, April 13, 2005.

5. Ana X. Ceron, "Labor Center Delivers Jobs, Calmer Streets," *Palm Beach Post*, September 4, 2007.

6. Mike Richmond, "El Sol Marks a Year of Success," *Jupiter Courier*, September 9, 2007.

7. "Jupiter's El Sol," *New York Times*, February 26, 2011.

8. The Guatemalan consulate closest to Jupiter is located approximately 90 miles south in Miami. Thus the consulate periodically offers consular services to Guatemalan citizens via mobile units dispatched to more easily accessible sites such as El Sol or Saint Peter Catholic Church.

9. "Man Acquitted in El Sol Scuffle," *Jupiter-Tequesta Hometown News*, March 28, 2008.

10. FLIMEN: Floridians for Immigration Enforcement, "Jupiter Illegal Alien Hiring Hall Protest Every Saturday, 9AM–Noon," http://www.flimen.org/JupiterProtests.htm (accessed July 6, 2012).

11. *Palm Beach Post*, front page, April 19, 2009.

12. Dan Moffet, "See Real People by the Light of El Sol," *Palm Beach Post*, May 11, 2008.

CHAPTER 5. THE EL SOL FAMILY

1. El Sol had a lottery system, using tickets to determine who went out to work in the early days before the computerized system went into place.

2. See Alejandro Portes and Rubén G. Rumbaut, *Legacies: The Story of the Immigrant Second Generation* (Berkeley: University of California Press, 2001), for an example of this literature.

CHAPTER 6. LOCAL SOLUTIONS AND IMPLICATIONS FOR THE NATIONAL IMMIGRATION DEBATE

1. Tamar Jacoby, "Immigration, Jobs, and the Economy," talk given at the Woodrow Wilson International Center for Scholars, Washington, D.C., June 8, 2010, http:// wilsoncenter.org/ondemand/index.cfm (accessed July 6, 2012).

2. Jeffrey Passel and D'Vera Cohn, "A Portrait of Unauthorized Immigrants in the United States," Pew Hispanic Center report, April 14, 2009, http://www.pewhispanic .org/files/reports/107.pdf (accessed July 6, 2012).

3. Gebe Martinez, "Unconstitutional and Costly: The High Price of Local Immigration Enforcement," Center for American Progress report, January 2011, http://www .americanprogress.org/wp-content/uploads/issues/2011/01/pdf/cost_of_enforcement .pdf (accessed July 6, 2012), 4.

4. Ibid., 16–17.

5. Ibid., 18.

6. Thomas Guterbock, Christopher Koper, Milton Vickerman, Bruce Taylor, Karen Walker, and Timothy Carter, "Evaluation Study of Prince William County's Illegal Immigration Enforcement Policy: Final Report 2010," report prepared by the University of Virginia Center for Survey Research and the Police Executive Research Forum for the Prince William County Police Department, November 2010, http://www.pwcgov .org/government/dept/police/Documents/13185.pdf (accessed July 6, 2012), xvi.

7. Ibid., xvii.

8. Robert Friedman, "Property Wasn't Bought Especially for Labor Center," letter to the editor, *Palm Beach Post*, March 24, 2008.

9. Rubén Rumbaut, Roberto Gonzales, Golnaz Komaie, and Charlie V. Morgan, "Debunking the Myth of Immigrant Criminality: Imprisonment among First- and Second-Generation Young Men," *Migration Information Resource*, June 2006, http:// www.migrationinformation.org/usfocus/display.cfm?ID=403 (accessed July 6, 2012).

10. Claude Fischer and Michael Hout, *Century of Difference: How America Changed in the Last One Hundred Years* (New York: Russell Sage Foundation, 2006), 43.

11. Abel Valenzuela, Nick Theodore, Edwin Melendez, and Ana Luz Gonzalez, "On the Corner: Day Labor in the United States," http://www.sscnet.ucla.edu/issr/csup/ uploaded_files/Natl_DayLabor-On_the_Corner1.pdf (accessed July 6, 2012), 12.

12. Ibid., 14.

13. FBI Uniform Crime Report Stats and Services, http://www.fbi.gov/about-us/cjis/ucr/crime-in-the-u.s/2010/crime-in-the-u.s.-2010/tables/table-8/10tbl08fl.xls (accessed July 6, 2012).

14. Janice Fine, *Worker Centers: Organizing Communities at the Edge of the Dream* (London and Ithaca: EPI and Cornell University Press, 2006), 3.

15. Monica Varsanyi, *Taking Local Control: Immigration Policy Activism in U.S. Cities and States* (Stanford: Stanford University Press, 2010), 3; National Immigration Law Center, "Laws, Resolutions, and Policies Instituted across the U.S. Limiting Enforcement of Immigration Laws by State and Local Authorities," National Immigration Law Center, December 2008, http://v2011.nilc.org/immlawpolicy/LocalLaw/locallaw-limiting-tbl-2008-12-03.pdf (accessed July 6, 2012).

16. Varsanyi, *Taking Local Control*, 67.

17. Ibid.

18. Robert Putnam, "*E Pluribus Unum*: Diversity and Community in the Twenty-first Century, the 2006 Johan Skytte Prize Lecture," *Journal of Scandinavian Political Studies* 30, no. 2 (June 2007): 137–74.

SUGGESTED READINGS

Unauthorized Immigration History and Causes

Kivisto, Peter, and Thomas Faist. *Beyond a Border: The Causes and Consequences of Contemporary Immigration*. Los Angeles: Pine Forge Press, 2010.

Marquardt, Marie F., Timothy J. Steigenga, Phillip J. Williams, and Manuel A. Vasquez. *Living "Illegal": The Human Face of Unauthorized Immigration*. New York: New Press, 2011.

Massey, Douglas S., Jorge Durand, and Nolan J. Malone. *Beyond Smoke and Mirrors: Mexican Immigration in an Era of Economic Integration*. New York: Russell Sage Foundation, 2002.

Massey, Douglas, and Kristin Espinosa. "What's Driving Mexico-US Migration? A Theoretical, Empirical, and Policy Analysis." *American Journal of Sociology* 102, no. 4 (1997): 939–99.

Ngai, Mae M. *Impossible Subjects: Illegal Aliens and the Making of Modern America*. Princeton, N.J.: Princeton University Press, 2004.

Portes, Alejandro, and Rubeìn G. Rumbaut. *Immigrant America: A Portrait*. Berkeley: University of California Press, 1996.

Ueda, Reed. *Postwar Immigrant America: A Social History*. Boston: Bedford Books of St. Martin's Press, 1994.

New Destinations and Transnationalism

Massey, Douglas S., ed. *New Faces in New Places: The Changing Geography of American Immigration*. New York: Russell Sage Foundation, 2008.

Odem, Mary E., and Elaine Cantrell Lacy, eds. *Latino Immigrants and the Transformation of the U.S. South*. Athens: University of Georgia Press, 2009.

Williams, Philip J., Timothy J. Steigenga, and Manuel A. Vaìsquez, eds. *A Place to Be: Brazilian, Guatemalan, and Mexican Immigrants in Florida's New Destinations*. New Brunswick, N.J.: Rutgers University Press, 2009.

Zúñiga, Víctor, and Rubén León. *New Destinations: Mexican Immigration in the United States*. New York: Russell Sage Foundation, 2005.

Day Labor and Worker Centers

Fine, Janice. *Worker Centers: Organizing Communities at the Edge of the Dream*. London and Ithaca: EPI and Cornell University Press, 2006.

National Day Laborer Organizing Network. http://www.ndlon.org.

Theodore, Nik, Abel Valenzuela, and Edwin Meléndez. "Worker Centers: Defending Labor Standards for Migrant Workers in the Informal Economy." *International Journal of Manpower* 30 (November 2011): 422–36.

Valenzuela, Abel. "Day Labor Work." *Annual Review of Sociology* 29 (2003): 307–33.

———. "Working on the Margins: Immigrant Day Labor Characteristics and Prospects for Employment." Working Paper 22. Center for Comparative Immigration Studies, May 2000.

Media, Rhetoric, and Representations of Immigrants

Bacon, David. *Illegal People: How Globalization Creates Migration and Criminalizes Immigrants*. Boston: Beacon Press, 2008.

Chavez, Leo R. *The Latino Threat: Constructing Immigrants, Citizens, and the Nation*. Stanford: Stanford University Press, 2008.

Chomsky, Aviva. *"They Take Our Jobs!" and 20 Other Myths about Immigration*. Boston: Beacon Press, 2007.

Immigrant Integration and Assimilation

Alba, Richard, and Victor Nee. *Remaking the American Mainstream: Assimilation and Contemporary Immigration*. Cambridge, Mass.: Harvard University Press, 2003.

Massey, Douglas S., and Magaly Sánchez. *Brokered Boundaries: Creating Immigrant Identity in Anti-immigrant Times*. New York: Russell Sage Foundation, 2010.

Portes, Alejandro, and Rubén G. Rumbaut. *Legacies: The Story of the Immigrant Second Generation*. Berkeley: University of California Press, 2001.

Rodriguez, Marc S. *The Tejano Diaspora: Mexican Americanism and Ethnic Politics in Texas and Wisconsin*. Chapel Hill: University of North Carolina Press in association with the William P. Clements Center for Southwest Studies, Southern Methodist University, 2011

Immigration Policy: National and Local

Cornelius, Wayne, and Idean Salehyan. "Does Border Enforcement Deter Unauthorized Immigration? The Case of Mexican Migration to the United States of America." *Regulation and Governance* 1 (2007): 139–53.

Furman, Rich, and Nalini Negi. *Social Work Practice with Latinos: Key Issues and Emerging Themes*. Chicago: Lyceum Books, 2010.

Hing, Bill Ong. *Defining America through Immigration Policy*. Philadelphia: Temple University Press, 2004.

Massey, Douglas S. "The Wall That Keeps Illegal Workers In." *New York Times*, April 4, 2006.

———. "Testimony of Douglas S. Massey before the Senate Judiciary Committee." Senate Judiciary Committee, May 20, 2009. http://www.judiciary.senate.gov/hearings/

testimony.cfm?id=e655f9e2809e5476862f735da149ad69&wit_id=e655f9e2809e547
6862f735da149ad69-2-4 (accessed February 6, 2012).

Varsanyi, Monica. *Taking Local Control: Immigration Policy Activism in U.S. Cities and States*. Stanford: Stanford University Press, 2010.

GUATEMALAN IMMIGRANTS, WORK, EXILE, AND COMMUNITY

Burns, Allan F. *Maya in Exile: Guatemalans in Florida*. Philadelphia: Temple University Press, 1993.

Fink, Leon. *The Maya of Morganton: Work and Community in the Nuevo New South*. Chapel Hill: University of North Carolina Press, 2003.

Gzesh, Suzan. "Central Americans and Asylum Policy in the Reagan Era." Migration Information Source, Migration Policy Institute, April 1 2006. http://www.migration information.org/Feature/display.cfm?id=384 (accessed February 6, 2012).

Hagan, Jacqueline Maria. *Deciding to Be Legal: A Maya Community in Houston*. Philadelphia: Temple University Press, 1994.

Montejo, Victor. *Voices from Exile: Violence and Survival in Modern Maya History*. Norman: University of Oklahoma Press, 1999.

Steigenga, Timothy, and Sandra Lazo de la Vega. "Guatemalan Immigrants." In *Multicultural America: An Encyclopedia of the Newest Americans*. Santa Barbara, Denver, and Oxford: Greenwood, 2011.

Thompson, Charles, dir. *Brother Towns: Pueblos Hermanos*. Center for Documentary Studies, Duke University, 2010. DVD.

INDEX